In the Light of the Lord

Weekday Reflections for Lent and Easter

In the Light of the Lord

Weekday Reflections for Lent and Easter

Ernest Ferlita, S.J.

ThomasMore®
– An RCL Company –
Allen, Texas

Acknowledgments

Excerpts from the English translation of *The Roman Missal* © 1973, International Committee on English in the Liturgy, Inc. (ICEL). All rights reserved.

The Scripture quotations contained herein, except for those noted in the text, are from the *New Revised Standard Version Bible: Catholic Edition* copyright © 1993 and 1989 by the Division of Christian Education for the National Council of the Churches of Christ in the U.S.A. Used by permission. All rights reserved.

References to quotations from the *Revised English Bible* are followed by REB; references from the *New Jerusalem Bible* by NJB.

Send all inquiries to:
Thomas More® Publishing
An RCL Company
200 East Bethany Drive
Allen, Texas 75002–3804

Telephone: 800-264-0368 / 972-390-6300
Fax: 800-688-8356 / 972-390-6560

Visit us at: **www.thomasmore.com**
Customer Service E-mail: **cservice@rcl-enterprises.com**

Printed in the United States of America

Library of Congress Control Number: 2002109704

7497   ISBN 0-88347-497-2

1 2 3 4 5   07 06 05 04 03

Contents

Foreword 9

Lent 11

Ash Wednesday   *The Dearest Freshness*
                     Deep Down Things 13
Thursday   *Choose Life, Lose Life* 15
Friday   *Fasting This Way and That* 17
Saturday   *The Compassion of God* 19

First Week of Lent
Monday   *God's Care* 21
Tuesday   *The Word of God* 23
Wednesday   *Sins of Collective Responsibility* 25
Thursday   *Prayer and Petition* 27
Friday   *The Ministry of Reconciliation* 29
Saturday   *The Enemy Destroyed* 31

Second Week of Lent
Monday   *The Power of God's Grace* 33
Tuesday   *Our Father, Who Art in Heaven* 36
Wednesday   *True Greatness* 38
Thursday   *The Rich and the Poor* 40
Friday   *A Foreshadowing of What*
                     Is to Come 42
Saturday   *The Father's Joy* 44

Third Week of Lent
Monday   *Acceptance and Rejection* 47
Tuesday   *Seventy Times Seven* 50
Wednesday   *The Path of Salvation* 52
Thursday   *Sins of the Spirit* 54
Friday   *The Mind of Christ* 56
Saturday   *The Love that God Desires* 58

Fourth Week of Lent

Monday	Signs of the New Life	61
Tuesday	Rivers of Living Water	63
Wednesday	Compassion Now and Always	65
Thursday	The Testimony of Good Works	67
Friday	Who Do People Say that I Am?	70
Saturday	The Way and the Truth and the Life	72

Fifth Week of Lent

Monday	Trust in the Lord	75
Tuesday	The Sign of the Cross	78
Wednesday	The Truth of the Matter	80
Thursday	The Preeminence of Christ	82
Friday	Throwing Stones	84
Saturday	God's People	86

Holy Week

Monday	The Fragrance of the Oil	89
Tuesday	The Giving of a Name	91
Wednesday	Betrayal	93
Holy Thursday	In the Upper Room	95
Good Friday	The Ultimate Epiphany	99

Easter ... 101

Easter Week

Monday	Praise the Lord	103
Tuesday	The Risen Lord	105
Wednesday	The Beautiful	107
Thursday	With the Eyes of the Soul	109
Friday	The Breaking of the Bread	111
Saturday	Not Seeing and Believing	113

Second Week of Easter

Monday	*Water and Spirit*	115
Tuesday	*Wind and Spirit*	117
Wednesday	*New Life*	119
Thursday	*The Penetrating Light of Christ*	121
Friday	*For the Sake of the Name*	123
Saturday	*Working for Those in Need*	126

Third Week of Easter

Monday	*The Work of God*	129
Tuesday	*God's Bread*	131
Wednesday	*Hunger and Thirst*	133
Thursday	*Faith Seeking Understanding*	135
Friday	*Holy Communion*	137
Saturday	*Faith and Love*	139

Fourth Week of Easter

Monday	*The Gate of God*	141
Monday (Yr A)	*Knowing and Loving*	143
Tuesday	*Eternal Life*	145
Wednesday	*Light from Light*	147
Thursday	*One and the Same*	149
Friday	*Embrace and Release*	151
Saturday	*To the Ends of the Earth*	153

Fifth Week of Easter

Monday	*Jesus Revealed*	157
Tuesday	*Peace*	159
Wednesday	*The Vine and the Branches*	161
Thursday	*The Cause of Our Joy*	163
Friday	*The Gift of God's Love*	165
Saturday	*The Light of the World*	167

Sixth Week of Easter

Monday	*Witness*	169
Tuesday	*The Presence of Christ through the Spirit.*	171
Wednesday	*The Spirit of Truth*	173
Ascension Thursday	*The Love that Moves the Sun*	175
Friday	*Open Wide the Doors to Christ*	177
Saturday	*Requests Made in the Name of Jesus.*	179

Seventh Week of Easter

Monday	*The Gift of the Spirit*	181
Tuesday	*Now and in the Future.*	183
Wednesday	*Consecration in Truth*	185
Thursday	*Life and Love*	187
Friday	*Love and Service*	189
Saturday	*Come, Holy Spirit!*	191

Works Cited 195

Scripture Index 199

Foreword

Jesus, as we say in the Creed, is Light from Light. To him too, therefore, we sing from the Psalms: "[I]n your light we see light" (36:9) and "The unfolding of your words gives light; it imparts understanding to the simple" (119:130). Because of this, I propose in the title that we reflect on the readings for the Weekdays of Lent and Easter "in the light of the Lord."

These reflections are offered to anyone hoping for a deeper faith and understanding. As Saint Paul says to the Ephesians: "Live as children of light—for the fruit of the light is found in all that is good and right and true. Try to find out what is pleasing to the Lord" (5:8–10).

They can be helpful to preachers too. I myself find it helpful to consult other books on the Word of God whenever I have to prepare a homily.

Lent

February 17th 2010

Ash Wednesday

Joel 2:12–18
2 Corinthians 5:20–6:2
Matthew 6:1–6, 16–18

The Dearest Freshness Deep Down Things

Lent is an old English word meaning springtime,
a time when the days began to lengthen.
It refers to the time of year, yes,
but it also says something about this time of penance.
Spring is twofold in character:
barrenness, darkness, death are still in evidence,
but *something is in motion.*
Spring is a time when what is hidden comes to light,
when what is seemingly dead comes to life,
when the earth takes in the rain and the sunlight
and awakens to its very depths.
"There lives the dearest freshness deep down things."
So says the poet Gerard Manley Hopkins.[1]
This freshness must struggle against incrustation,
overcrowding, pollution.
Nature is partly to blame,
and nature partly assists in the struggle.
We humans are partly to blame—
through greed, indifference, exploitation—
and we partly assist—through discipline,
regulation, the curbing of destructive instincts.
Somehow the freshness of things breaks through,
and behold, there is renewal.

---

[1] *God's Grandeur.*

In the Light of the Lord　　　13

Lent for us is a time like that,
a struggle against darkness,
sluggishness, self-indulgence;
a struggle against the crowding out
of what is good and fresh and bright in us.
How? Through almsgiving, prayer, fasting.
~~These are the three religious acts~~
~~that Jesus brings up in today's gospel.~~ Jesus says
Give alms, pray, fast.
But don't be a hypocrite, he says,
don't make a point of putting on a show for others.
The temptation is to do the right thing
for the wrong reasons, as St. Thomas Becket
discovered in T. S. Eliot's *Murder in the Cathedral*.
All of our Lenten practices
must be done for the right reasons.

Paul in the second reading suggests
what these right reasons might be:
". . . on behalf of Christ, be reconciled to God."
Become "the righteousness of God" in him. (5:20–21)
Do not "accept the grace of God in vain" (6:1).

May this Lent be a time when, like the earth,
we take in the rain and the sunlight of God's love
and awaken to our very depths. [2]   AMEN

---

[2]Adapted from the author's *The Path of Life, Cycle A*, 43–44.

In the Light of the Lord

Thursday   *Deuteronomy 30:15–20*
                                               Luke 9:22–25

Choose Life, Lose Life

"Choose life," we heard Moses say in the first reading.
In the gospel Jesus says, "Lose your life for my sake."
How are we to understand this seeming contradiction?
Obviously it has to do with what is meant by life
in one context and the other.
Moses says: If you obey the commandments,
if you love God, you are choosing life.
Choosing to obey, choosing to love God,
is certainly not choosing a life that is self-centered,
but rather a life of compassion,
a life of concern for others.
But when Jesus says, If you desire to save your life,
he is indeed referring to a life that is self-centered.
So if you save your self-centered life,
you lose your life,
not just your eternal life, your life with God,
but life here and now, life that leads to eternal life.
But if you *lose* your self-centered life, you *gain* life.
Which is another way of saying:
"[T]hose who lose their life for my sake will save it" (Luke 9:24).

Lent is certainly a time to consider
how well we've done, or how well we're doing,
at losing our self-centered life in order to gain life.
But Lent is not necessarily a time
for giving up more things than usual,

for making things more difficult for ourselves.
No, it's not that. As Pope John Paul said,
"[This] period that leads to Easter
represents a providential gift of the Lord
and a precious opportunity to draw closer to him,
turning inward and listening to his voice within us."[3]
Lent, I think we can say, is a journey
toward the life of the risen Lord.

The life that Moses had in mind
when he said, "Choose life,"
and that Jesus urged us to adopt
in order to follow him
is, of course, a life of action,
of doing things in the light of the Lord.
That's why today's opening prayer
is very apt and worth repeating:
"Lord, may everything we do
begin with your inspiration,
continue with your help,
and reach perfection under your guidance."

---

[3]From the Vatican, 7 February 2001.

In the Light of the Lord

Friday

Isaiah 58:1–9
Matthew 9:14–15

Fasting This Way and That

"Why do we fast?" Isaiah raises this question.
Fasting is the theme of both readings.
But how are we to understand fasting?
Is fasting just giving up something to eat?

In the light of the gospel,
maybe one reason we fast is to experience hunger,
not just hunger in the physical sense
but in the spiritual sense as well: hunger for God.

So long as the bridegroom is with them, why fast?
But "when the bridegroom is taken away from them,
. . . then they will fast" (9:15).
Jesus speaks of fasting as a sign of mourning.
One mourns over someone gone.
Implicit in the act of mourning is desire,
even love, for the one gone.

But the one gone, which in this case
is none other than Jesus, identifies himself
with others who are still with us:
"[F]or I was hungry and you gave me food,
I was thirsty and you gave me something to drink . . .
Truly I tell you, just as you did it
to one of the least of these

In the Light of the Lord   17

who are members of my family,
you did it to me" (Matthew 25:35, 40).

This corresponds exactly with the fasting
that the Lord expects of us, according to Isaiah.
The fasting he expects of us
is releasing those bound unjustly,
letting the oppressed go free,
sharing bread with the hungry,
sheltering the homeless poor,
clothing the naked,
and not turning away from your own kin.

Fasting, in this sense,
is extending one's self for others,
extending one's self for others
like all the saints and martyrs.

"Then your light," says the Lord,
"shall break forth like the dawn,
and your healing shall spring up quickly. . . .
Then you shall call, and the LORD will answer,
you shall cry for help,
and he will say: Here I am!" (58:8–9)

In the Light of the Lord

Saturday

Isaiah 58:9–14
Luke 5:27–32

The Compassion of God

Today's first reading from Isaiah starts
with the second half of the same verse
that ended yesterday's reading,
and it amplifies much the same idea.
"If you remove the [oppression from your midst],
the pointing of the finger,
the speaking of evil,
if you offer your food to the hungry
and satisfy the needs of the afflicted;
then light shall rise in the darkness
and your gloom be like the noonday" (58:9–10).
The point is that merely external things,
like ritual, like fasting, are not enough;
these things must be joined by internal things,
like mercy, compassion, sincerity.

How does this relate to the Pharisees?
As we often meet them in the Gospels,
they are so obsessed with ritual and law
that they never open themselves to God's mercy,
and as a result they never learn to be merciful.
In today's gospel they complain to the disciples:
"Why do you eat and drink
with tax collectors and sinners?"
And it's Jesus, not the disciples,
who replies: "Those who are well

In the Light of the Lord　　　19

have no need of a physician,
but those who are sick;
I have come to call not the righteous
but sinners to repentance" (5:30–32).
Of course, when he says "the righteous"
he's speaking ironically.
The righteous can be sinners too
if they never show mercy to others.

"Jesus has been called 'the compassion of God.'"[4]
By joining sinners at table,
"he revealed himself to them
in the depths of their own hearts,"
forgave them their sins,
and "set them on a path of new life."[5]

As we prayed in the opening prayer,
may God "look upon our weakness,"
and through his son Jesus Christ
"reach out to help us with [his] loving power."

---

[4]Monika Hellwig, *Jesus the Compassion of God*, quoted by C. M. LaCugna, *God for Us*, 294.
[5]LaCugna, *God for Us*, 294.

In the Light of the Lord

Monday

Leviticus 19:1–2, 11–18
Matthew 25:31–46

God's Care

In the gospel for the first Sunday of Lent
Jesus is tempted by Satan in the desert.
The conflict doesn't begin with temptation,
and it doesn't end there.
It begins, we might say, when the human race begins,
and it ends at the Last Judgment.
Since both the temptations and the Last Judgment
are told in mythic or parabolic form,
it may be helpful to look to a mythic tale
for the beginning of that conflict.
Here's a Mormon version of the myth.[6]
Both Christ and Lucifer are required to present God
with a plan for dealing with the infant human race.
Lucifer reminds God that he has armies of angels
at his command: "Just assign one to each human being
with power to punish: That should keep them in line."
Christ, for his part, says:
"Let them have free will and go their way,
but allow me to live and die as one of them,
both to show them how to live
and how much you care for them."

God, of course, chose Christ's plan.
Christ came to show us how to live

---

[6]As told in M. Scott Peck's *People of the Lie.*

and to show us how much God cares for us
and showed us how to care for others.

In the first reading from Leviticus
God expresses that care in the form of commandments.
"You shall not steal . . . you shall not lie. . . .
You shall not defraud your neighbor,"
ending with "you shall love your neighbor as yourself."

In the gospel's account of the Last Judgment,
the righteous ones show surprise
at God's rewarding them for what they have done;
what they did was care for others
with no thought of personal compensation.
They learned their lesson well,
how much God cares for us
and how our care for others is patterned on his;
how we are judged precisely for our compassion
or lack thereof.

Tuesday

Isaiah 55:10–11
Matthew 6:7–15

The Word of God

As we heard in the first reading from Isaiah,
rain and snow come down from the heavens
but do not return till they have watered the earth
and made it fertile and fruitful.
And so shall my word be, God says,
the word that "goes out from my mouth;
it shall not return to me empty,
but it shall accomplish [what] I purpose,
and succeed in the thing for which I sent it" (55:11).

The first meaning of God's word
is obviously his message to us.
But the fullest meaning of God's word
is Jesus Christ, the Word made flesh (John 1:14).
He knew "that he had come from God
and was going to God" (John 13:3).
He would not return void,
but would do God's will,
achieving the end for which God sent him.

And one of the great petitions
that Jesus teaches us to pray,
as we heard him say in the "Our Father,"
is very explicit about doing God's will:
"Your will be done,
on earth as it is in heaven."

Almost all the Fathers of the Church
comment on this petition.
Origen says, "In committing ourselves to [Christ],
we can become one spirit with him,
and thereby accomplish [God's] will,
in such wise that it will be perfect
on earth as it is in heaven."
And Saint John Chrysostom asks us to consider
how Jesus "commands each of the faithful who prays
to do so universally, for the whole world.
For he did not say 'Thy will be done in me or in us,'
but 'on the earth,' the whole earth,
so that error may be banished from it,
truth take root in it,
all vice be destroyed on it,
virtue flourish on it,
and earth no longer differ from heaven."[7]

That is "a consummation devoutly to be wished."[8]
And to be prayed for daily.
But it's not something that can be answered in a day.
Unlike the next petition, which can be:
"Give us this day our daily bread"—
the bread of nourishment that life requires,
for us to enjoy and to share with others,
but above all, "the Bread of Life:
the Word of God accepted in faith,
the Body of Christ received in the Eucharist."[9]

---

[7]*Catechism of the Catholic Church*, 2nd ed., #2825.
[8]*Hamlet*, III, 1, 56.
[9]*Catechism of the Catholic Church*, 2nd ed., #2835

Wednesday

Jonah 3:1–10
Luke 11:29–32

Sins of Collective Responsibility

Jonah is a very reluctant prophet.
In spite of God's mercy,
he wants to see the Ninevites perish.
But lo and behold, they repent.
What do they repent of? Of their evil ways,
as their king declared in the first reading,
and the violence they have in their hands.
Why do they repent?

In the gospel Jesus, one who is greater than Jonah,
addresses the crowd that gathers around him.
This is an "evil generation," he says (11:29).
But unlike the Ninevites they will not repent.
Why? Why will they not repent?

Dr. Karl Meninger, who has been called
the Dean of American psychiatry,
wrote a book entitled *Whatever Became of Sin?*
He is troubled by individuals
who won't admit that they sin.
He also refers to "sins of collective responsibility"—
sins committed by groups or nations,
such as disregard for the poor,
pollution of the environment,
exploitation of migrant workers.
The tragic thing, he says,

about "sins of collective responsibility,"
is that single individuals
don't consider themselves responsible for them.

In the story of Jonah and the Ninevites,
the Ninevites are addressed as a nation.
Their sins, therefore, must include
sins of collective responsibility.
And they repent. The king and individual citizens
admit their responsibility.

What about the "evil generation" that Jesus addresses?
Are they also guilty of sins
of collective responsibility?
In Monday's gospel about the judgment of the nations,
Jesus said to those on his left:
"I was hungry and you gave me no food,
I was thirsty and you gave me nothing to drink . . . ,"
concluding with this declaration:
"[J]ust as you did not do it to one of the least of these,
you did not do it to me" (Matthew 25:42–45).

Well, as we say in the verse before the gospel,
"If today you hear his voice
harden not your hearts."

Thursday   *Esther C:12, 14–16, 23–25*
                                                      Matthew 7:7–12

Prayer and Petition

Queen Esther asked and she received.
She prayed to God for "help," "courage,"
and "persuasive words" (C:24:14, 23, 24).
She didn't then just sit back and wait.
She went to the king and persuaded him
to rescue her people from their enemy.
It was prayer that fueled her action.

God knows our needs even before we ask (Matthew 6:8).
That doesn't mean, don't ask.
On the contrary, as we heard Jesus say,
"Ask, and it will be given you" (Matthew 7:7).
In asking, we learn to distinguish
between wants and needs.
When I pray for this or that,
are these wants or needs?
It's not always easy to distinguish.[10]
We feel at times we need more recognition,
more money, more success in what we do.
If these things come, they may bring further problems.
As Saint Teresa of Avila is supposed to have said,
More tears are shed over answered prayers
than unanswered prayers.

---

[10]See Gerard W. Hughes, *O God Why?*, 77.

In the Light of the Lord   27

But God will not give a stone if we ask for bread,
or a serpent if we ask for fish.
God desires our good.
We must trust in God's goodness.
As we prayed in the opening prayer,
"Father, without you we can do nothing."
Which is one way of saying
that God is our greatest need.
"By your Spirit help us to know what is right
and to be eager in doing your will."

"In his will is our peace." [11]
As Saint Paul says in Philippians:
"The Lord is near.
Do not worry about anything, but in everything
by prayer and supplication with thanksgiving
let your requests be made known to God.
and the peace of God,
which surpasses all understanding,
will guard your hearts and your minds
in Christ Jesus" (4:5–7).

---

[11]Dante, *Paradiso*, III.

Friday

Ezekiel 18:21–28
Matthew 5:20–26

The Ministry of Reconciliation

Be reconciled with yourself and with one another,
if you want to be reconciled with me.
That, in effect, is what God is saying
in today's readings.
According to Saint Paul, God has given us
"the ministry of reconciliation" (2 Corinthians 5:18).
Reconciliation is very hard to achieve
when both sides in a conflict
feel that they are in the right.
The hope is that eventually one side
will admit more wrong than the other.
What does it mean to be a minister of reconciliation
when *my* side is in the wrong?
What does it mean when the other side is in the wrong?

Jesus answers the first question in today's gospel.
"[When] you are offering your gift at the altar," he says,
"if you remember that your brother or sister
has something against you,
leave your gift there before the altar and go;
first be reconciled with your brother or sister,
and then come and offer your gift" (5:23–24).
In other words, how can you be reconciled with God
if you refuse to be reconciled
with your brother or sister?
Jesus is saying that if I know I am wrong,

In the Light of the Lord   29

it is for me to make the first move.
A minister of reconciliation, then,
is humble enough to ask forgiveness.

What does it mean to be a minister of reconciliation
when the other side is wrong? Later on,
in the same chapter from Matthew as today's gospel,
Jesus says, "You have heard that it was said,
'An eye for an eye and a tooth for a tooth.'
But I say to you, Do not resist an evildoer.
But if anyone strikes you on the right cheek,
turn the other also" (5:38–39).
This saying is often misunderstood.
Why does Jesus say turn the other cheek?
"A wolf has enlightened me,"
says Konrad Lorenz in his book on animal ways.[12]
When two wolves get into a fight,
the one that finds himself backed into a corner
will immediately bend his neck
and offer his jugular vein to the other.
And the other will not attack.
By making himself vulnerable,
the cornered wolf apparently disarms the attacker.
Now what wolves do by instinct, human beings,
in the complexity of their freedom,
must learn to do by grace.
When Jesus tells you to turn the other cheek,
the reason is not to let your enemy strike you again,
but to make him unable to do so.

A minister of reconciliation, then, does not resist evil,
that is, you do not offer insult for insult;
you yield to grace and try to make room for grace
in the heart of the attacker.

---

[12]*King Solomon's Ring*, 209.

All this is to say that a minister of reconciliation
is a minister of God's Spirit—
a Spirit of truth, forgiveness, and love.[13]

Saturday   *Deuteronomy 26:16–19*
                                Matthew 5:43–48

The Enemy Destroyed

Pope John Paul has apologized and asked forgiveness
for all the sins of our past life.
I mean the past life of every member of the church,
going back hundreds of years.
What the pope was asking forgiveness for
is, in a way, the failure of Christians
to live what Jesus commands in today's gospel:
"Love your enemies
and pray for those who persecute you" (5:44).

This is too much for some people.
They become outraged,
like a woman from somewhere in the North
who wrote to Abraham Lincoln when she heard
that he had released a southern soldier from prison
so he could work on his needy mother's farm:

---

[13]Adapted from the author's *The Way of the River,* 27–29.

"You don't free your enemies," she said;
"you destroy them."
"Madam," he replied, "if I make my enemy my friend,
don't I destroy my enemy?"[14]
Exactly what Jesus meant.

Were the Israelites told to hate their enemy?
It certainly wasn't one of the ten commandments,
but according to Jesus in the gospel,
they were told to hate their enemy.
In today's first reading from the Book of Deuteronomy
we heard Moses tell the people
that the Lord is making an agreement with them,
that they are to be a people "peculiarly his own,"
that the Lord will raise them high in praise
and renown and glory above all other nations.
That certainly makes them special,
but it does not command them to hate all others.
And yet in the same Book of Deuteronomy
Moses tells the people: "When the LORD your God
brings you into the land
that you are about to enter and occupy,"
when he drives out many nations before you
and delivers them into your power,
"then you must utterly destroy them" (7:1–2).

Yes, to be God's people is to be special.
But, as Jesus puts it, to be special is to be like God.
"Be perfect," he says,
"as your heavenly Father is perfect" (5:48).

¹⁴Quoted in Herbert F. Smith, S.J., *Sunday Homilies,* Cycle A. 53.

In the Light of the Lord

Monday

Daniel 9:4–10
Luke 6:36–38

The Power of God's Grace

"Forgive and you will be forgiven" (Luke 6:37).
To forgive: that, from a certain point of view,
is the essence of the gospel.
This, in a sense, is what Jesus is all about,
in both word and deed.
His very presence in our midst
is the expression of the Father's compassion.
"Be compassionate, as your Father is compassionate,"
another way of translating
what we hear in today's gospel:
"Be merciful, just as your Father is merciful" (6:36).

Several years ago, in the national news,
there was a story of reconciliation
between Cardinal Bernardin of Chicago
and Steven Cook, a former seminarian,
who had falsely accused him of sexual abuse.
Bernardin had requested a meeting with his accuser,
"to let him know," he said,
"that I harbor no ill feelings towards him,
and to pray with him
for his physical and spiritual well-being."
Steven Cook apologized for the embarrassment
and the hurt he had caused.
His apology, Bernardin said,

"was simple, direct, moving.
I told him that while I would not want
to go through such a humiliating experience again,
it had contributed to my own spiritual growth
and had made me more compassionate."
When Steven said he felt alienated
from God and Church,
Bernardin said he would not press the issue
but he wanted to show him two things.
The first thing was a Bible he had brought as a gift.
Steven clutched it tightly to his chest.
Then Bernardin showed him a chalice
that someone had sent him for Mass.
"Please," Steven said, "let's celebrate Mass."
And this is the Cardinal's final comment:
"Never in my forty-three years as a priest
have I witnessed a more profound reconciliation.
The words I am using to tell you this story
cannot begin to describe the power of God's grace
which was at work that afternoon.
It was a manifestation of God's love,
forgiveness and healing which I will never forget."[15]

Forgiveness is not easy,
especially when the one to be forgiven
has become one's enemy.
"[L]ove your enemies and do good to them . . ." (6:35).
Martin Luther King, Jr. felt that loving one's enemies
was an absolute necessity for our survival,
and therefore the key to the solution
of the problems of our world.
But it is "impossible," he said, "even to begin the act
of loving one's enemies without the prior acceptance

---

[15]*Clarion Herald*, February 2, 1995.

In the Light of the Lord

of the necessity, over and over again,
of forgiving those who inflict evil and injury upon us.
It is also necessary to realize that the forgiving act
must always be initiated by the person
who has been wronged, the victim of some great hurt,
the recipient of some tortuous injustice,
the absorber of some terrible act of oppression."[16]
And Martin Luther King knew
by bitter experience whereof he spoke.

All the more reason to take to heart
these last words of Jesus in today's gospel:
"Give, and there will be gifts for you:
a full measure, pressed down, shaken together,
and overflowing, will be poured into your lap" (6:38 NJB).

[16]*Richer Fare*, 160.

Tuesday

Isaiah 1:10, 16–20
Matthew 23:1–12

Our Father, Who Art in Heaven

"[C]all no one your father on earth,
for you have one Father—the one in heaven" (Matthew 23:9).
If one were to take this as an absolute statement,
without regard to context, then it would mean
not addressing even one's physical father as "Father."
But Jesus is talking about titles of respect,
such as the other two he mentions,
"Rabbi" and "Master."
Does he mean to totally prohibit the use of "Father"
as a title of respect? There are those who think so,
and some who are given the title
are not always comfortable with it.
But is Jesus actually saying, don't use it?
It sounds like it: "[C]all no one your father on earth,
for you have one Father—the one in heaven."

Earlier, Jesus said something similar to the rich man
who came up to him and said, "Good Teacher,
what must I do to inherit eternal life?"
And Jesus answered him, "Why do you call me good?
No one is good but God alone" (Mark 10:17–18).
What are we to make of this?
Are we really prohibited from calling anyone good,
even Jesus? I think not; I think Jesus is saying here,
and reminding us forcefully,
that the source of all goodness is God and God alone.

In the Light of the Lord

So, too, all fatherhood has its origin in God.
"All life, all holiness" comes from him,
we say in Eucharistic Prayer III.
Therefore, call no one on earth your father
if the truth that "you have one Father—the one in heaven"
is in any way diminished.

In his encyclical *On the Mercy of God* (II, 3),
Pope John Paul wrote: "Through his lifestyle
and through his actions, Jesus revealed . . .
an effective love, a love that addresses itself to [us]
and embraces everything that makes up our humanity . . .
Christ, then, reveals God who is Father, who is 'love' . . .
Making the Father present as love and mercy is . . .
the fundamental touchstone of [Christ's] mission."[17]

In other words, when Jesus says,
"You have one Father—the one in heaven,"
he's also saying, "And that Father is loving."
This being so, what does it mean for his children,
what does it mean for us, that is,
in our dealings with each other?
It means, of course, that we must love one another.[18]

---

[17]Quoted in *The Word Among Us*, Lent 2000, 35.
[18]Adapted, in part, from the author's *The Paths of Life*, Cycle A, 177–179.

Wednesday

Jeremiah 18:18–20
Matthew 20:17–28

True Greatness

In the overture to an opera
we get a foretaste of themes
that will be developed in full in a later act.
In today's readings, four weeks before Spy Wednesday,
so called because of Judas's plot to betray Jesus,
we get a foretaste of the theme
that will dominate Holy Week,
the suffering and death of Jesus Christ.

In the first reading, some six hundred years before Jesus,
the men of Judah contrive a plot against Jeremiah,
the prophet whose "career spanned the troubled years
which ended in the destruction of Jerusalem."[19]
Jeremiah begs God to heed his prayer:
"Is evil a recompense for good?
Yet [my adversaries] have dug a pit for my life.
Remember how I stood before you
to speak good for them,
to turn away your wrath from them" (18:20).

In today's gospel Jesus gives his apostles a preview
of his approaching passion and death;
it's "the most detailed of the three predictions

---

[19]John L. McKenzie, S.J., *Dictionary of the Bible*, 420.

made before the entry into Jerusalem."[20]
Departing from the previous traditions,
Matthew replaces "they will kill him"
with the exact "to be . . . crucified" (20:19).
And the role of the Gentiles is uttered
for the first time: he will be handed over to them.

How do the apostles react?
Well, other things are sounding in their ears.
John and James, Zebedee's sons,
come up to Jesus with their mother
and she does homage to Jesus and asks of him a favor.
"Declare that these two sons of mine will sit,
one at your right hand and one at your left,
in your kingdom" (20:21).
(Mark has the two sons themselves ask that favor;
maybe Matthew has the mother do it
to take some of the blame off James and John).[21]
Jesus, in response, addresses her and the two sons:
"You do not know what you are asking.
Are you able to drink the cup that I am about to drink?" (20:22)
Matthew's account of this incident "points forward
to his account of the Last Supper, when Jesus
[invites] all those present to share in his cup.
'. . . Drink from this, all of you; for this is my blood
of the covenant, . . . poured out for many
for the forgiveness of sins' " (26:27–28) (NJB).[22]

When the other apostles become indignant
at the two brothers, Jesus tells them
in no uncertain terms what true greatness is all about.
"[W]hoever wishes to be great among you

[20]John P. Meier, *Matthew*, 226.
[21]See Oliver McTernan's *A Call to Witness*, 90.
[22]Oliver McTernan, *A Call to Witness*, 94.

must be your servant,
and whoever wishes to be first among you
must be your slave; just as the Son of Man
came not to be served but to serve,
and to give his life a ransom for many" (20:26–28).

May the Lord plant in our hearts
the seeds of true greatness.

Thursday

Jeremiah 17:5–10
Luke 16:19–31

The Rich and the Poor

Dives and Lazarus, rich man and poor man.
The rich man is condemned, the poor man is blessed.
Actually, the parable gives no indication
that Dives "was guilty of moral wrong
or, for that matter, that Lazarus was morally right."[23]
Is the rich man condemned simply because he's rich?
Is the poor man blessed simply because he's poor?
It may seem so, but Dives is condemned
for ignoring the poor, for not listening
to Moses and the prophets concerning the poor.
And Lazarus is blessed, I think we can say,
for recognizing his need for God, for listening
to Moses and the prophets concerning the needy.

[23]*New Jerome Biblical Commentary,* 709.

In the Light of the Lord

As we hear the Lord say in the first reading
from the book of the prophet Jeremiah:
"I the LORD test the mind
    and search the heart,
to give to all according to their ways,
    according to the fruit of their doings" (17:10).

The thrust of the parable is certainly toward Dives,
toward the rich ignoring the poor.
How does this resonate with society today?
Are the rich richer and the poor poorer?
Not so long ago there was an interview with a person
in charge of school lunches in the State of Kentucky.
Some kids, she said, after school lunch on Friday
do not eat again till Monday!
I wonder if that's still the situation. I would hope not!

There's a website that some of you may be aware of—
thehungersite.com—a website that tells us
that every 3.6 seconds
someone somewhere in the world
dies of hunger. And 75 percent are children.
It shows us where, by darkening
the country on a map of the world.
If once a day you click there on the screen,
some help is given these countries
with donations paid for by various companies.

May the Spirit enable us to pray, work, vote
"to put right the structures and attitudes
which keep Dives feasting, while Lazarus starves."[24]

---

[24]*O God, Why?*, 91.

Friday
Genesis 37:3–4, 12–13, 17–28
Matthew 21:33–43, 45–46

A Foreshadowing of What is to Come

Some introductory comments for today's Mass
in the *Vatican II Weekday Missal* are worth noting.
This Friday is four weeks before Good Friday,
and today's readings, filled with thoughts
of suffering and death, have been used
for over a thousand years in this Lenten Mass.
Both of them point to Jesus' passion and death.

But the last part of the opening prayer
has us look over and beyond Christ's passion and death:
May everything we do
"open our hearts to [God's] love, and prepare us
for the coming feast of the resurrection."

In the first reading we're told the story
of Joseph and his brothers—Joseph,
whom his father Israel loved best of all.
Israel was the name given to Jacob
when he wrestled with an angel.
When Joseph's brothers see that their father
loves him more than them, they plot to kill him—
except for Reuben, the oldest, who says, Don't kill him,
just throw him into that cistern there.
Then another brother, Judah, has them sell him
for twenty pieces of silver

In the Light of the Lord

to some Ishmaelites passing by. Years later,
when Joseph becomes chief steward in Egypt
and his famished brothers come looking for grain,
Joseph whom they do not recognize at first,
reveals himself to them and says,
"[D]o not be distressed,
or angry with yourselves, because you sold me here;
for God sent me before you to preserve life" (Genesis 45:5).

In the parable of today's gospel a landowner
who had leased his vineyard to tenants
sends some of his servants
to get his share of the grapes.
The tenants abuse and kill them all,
and when the landowner sends his son
they kill him too.
Jesus tells this parable
just before he enters Jerusalem.
It's clearly a foreshadowing of Good Friday.
But also of the resurrection,
because he concludes the parable with these words:
"The stone that the builders rejected
has become the cornerstone;
this was the Lord's doing,
and it is [wonderful] in our eyes" (Matthew 21:42).

We can do bad things, and bad things can be done to us,
but the hope is that God in his providence
will restore and revive and replenish our lives.
We pray again what we prayed before:
May everything we do
"open our hearts to [God's] love, and prepare us
for the coming feast of the resurrection."

Saturday

Micah 7:14–15, 18–20
Luke 15:1–3, 11–32

The Father's Joy

Today's parable is one of three
that Jesus addressed to the scribes and Pharisees
when they began to complain about his welcoming
tax collectors and sinners,
and even going so far as to eat with them.
The parable of the lost sheep, of the lost coin,
and now the parable of the lost son
or, as it's generally called, The Prodigal Son,
prodigal meaning wasteful or extravagant.
The main focus of the story, however, is on the father,
so if we were to retitle it,
we might consider calling it "The Father's Joy."

The first two parables point us in this direction.
We're to identify
with the man who finds the lost sheep,
with the woman who finds the lost coin.
Wouldn't you go out to find that sheep, Jesus says,
wouldn't you light a lamp and sweep the house
in order to search for that coin?
And then when the sheep or the coin is found,
you'd tell everybody about it in your joy
and say, Rejoice with me!

So with the father in the third parable.
But there's a difference.
The father doesn't go in search of his son.
He makes no special effort to entice him back.
But the desire for his son's return is clearly there.
"[W]hile he was still far off,
his father saw him . . ." (Luke 15:20).
How often he had looked down that road!

Desire. This word comes from *sidus, sideris,*
a Latin word meaning "star." Odd, isn't it?
Why should desire derive from star?
To denote the reach of desire?
A reach as far as the stars.
At any rate, the father's desire
reaches into the heart of his son.
When the son comes to his senses,
he senses this desire and is drawn back.
Yes, if that desire could speak,
Come home! it would say.

The fulfillment of that desire
is the cause of the father's joy.
Celebrate! Rejoice!
The elder son will have none of it.
At this point Jesus' listeners are forced to look
through another character's eyes.
At first it was through the eyes of the father.
But now an elder son appears on the scene,
and he's furious when he finds out
what the music and dancing is all about.
The Pharisees can't help but see themselves in him.
Like the Pharisees who murmured against Jesus
for welcoming sinners, the elder son flares up

at his father for welcoming back his prodigal son.
The father says to him, "Son,
you are always with me,
and all that is mine is yours.
But we had to celebrate and rejoice,
because this brother of yours was dead
and has come to life;
he was lost and has been found" (15:31–32).

Where is Jesus in all this?
"I am in the Father," Jesus once said,
"and the Father is in me" (John 14:10).
Jesus manifests the Father to us,
never so clearly as in this parable.
The parable is a picture of how he, Jesus, acts,
and how he acts is how his Father acts.
The Father's desire reaches to us
through the heart of Christ—"Come home!" it says—
and then reaches through us to others, so that we too
become instruments of the Father's joy.[25]

---

[25]Adapted from the author's *The Paths of Life, Cycle C,* 52–55.

In the Light of the Lord

Monday

2 Kings 5:1–15
Luke 4:24–30

Acceptance and Rejection

All the turmoil in the Middle East
keeps us interested in its geography and its history.
The relationship between Israel and Syria
goes back a long way.
Syria was Aram of the first reading.
(The Aramaic dialect, the dialect that Jesus spoke,
originated there and was carried
into many parts of Palestine.)
Aram would sometimes ally itself with Israel
against the Assyrians, present-day Iraq,
but it was also a predatory neighbor.
When the king of Israel gets a note
from the king of Aram
concerning Naaman his army commander,
as we heard in the first reading, he thinks
the king of Aram is picking a quarrel with him.

Aram apparently made raids now and then:
the little girl, we're told, was captured in one of them
and became the servant of Naaman's wife.
Were her parents killed? We're not told.
But she seems to be fairly adjusted to her situation;
she tells her mistress about the prophet Elisha,
how he could cure Naaman of his leprosy.

What we have here is an image of God
drawing good out of evil, making evil work into good.

There were always Jews in Syria.
There were in Jesus' time and there are today.
After the persecution
following the stoning of Stephen,
Christians fled to Antioch in Syria. It was there
that they first began to be called Christians.
Luke is thought to have been born in Antioch
of a Greek-speaking pagan family,
and he wrote for the Gentile Christians there.
Jesus' mission to the Gentiles
is prominent in Luke's gospel.
Like Elijah and Elisha,
Jesus was not sent only for the Jews.

Today's gospel is the second part of an account in Luke
when Jesus goes into the synagogue in Nazareth
and reads a passage from Isaiah:
"The Spirit of the Lord is upon me,
because he has anointed me
to bring good news to the poor," etc.,
"and to proclaim the year
of the Lord's favor" (4:18–19).
This passage, he says, is fulfilled in your hearing.
The people are amazed.
"Is not this Joseph's son?" they say.
But then, abruptly, they reject him.
What's happening?
Luke has combined two episodes to show at the outset
the theme of acceptance/rejection.
And the hinge is this question: Is not this Joseph's son?
As a conclusion to the first part it denotes amazement.

As introduction to the second part
it comes across as a form of categorizing:
This is Joseph's son;
Jesus therefore is unable to reveal himself:
"no prophet is accepted in his own native place" (4:24).
They categorize him, pigeon-hole him.
Something that Jesus is always up against—
with them, and even with us.
Yes, to some extent that tendency is in us too:
not to accept a person on his or her own terms
but to categorize: on the basis of family,
social standing, race, nationality, religion.
"He's such and such . . ." "She comes from . . ."
And so on and so forth.
These so-called categories of knowing—
not knowing really—block love, lead even to hatred,
a hatred strong enough to kill.

As in the gospel, Jesus is driven out of town
and led to the brow of the hill,
down which they intend to hurl him,
but he passes through their midst and goes away.
This foreshadows the rejection of Holy Week,
his death and resurrection.
God drawing good out of evil,
making evil work into good.

"God of mercy," we pray again, "guide us,
for we cannot be saved without you."

Tuesday   *Daniel 3:25, 34–43*
                              Matthew 18:21–35

Seventy Times Seven

Forgiveness is never easy.
It's certainly not our first impulse.
It's not the way of the world we live in.
Surely there's a limit to the number of times
we're expected to forgive.
"[S]even times?" Peter asks Jesus in today's gospel.
Not "seven times," Jesus answers,
but "seventy times seven" (18:21–22 REB).
Which means there's no limit to forgiving.

Limiting our forgiveness limits us too.
In the parable that Jesus tells to enforce his point,
the steward is forgiven a huge debt.
But then he turns right around
and lays into someone who owes him a paltry sum.
As a result of his action,
the unforgiving steward is handed over to the jailers.
And we're told our Father in heaven
will treat us in exactly the same way
unless we forgive our brothers from our hearts.

At first, this may seem to contradict what Jesus says.
If God punishes us for not forgiving,
isn't God showing a lack of forgiveness?
The point is, however, "that being unforgiving,"

according to a pyschospiritual therapist,
"puts us in a jail of our own making.
Nobody suffers as much from nurtured resentments
as the person who harbors them. Hatred consumes
not the object of our scorn, but ourselves."[26]
In other words, by refusing
to open our hearts to others,
we close them to God's grace.
As the prophet Sirach says,
"Forgive your neighbor the wrong he has done,
and then your sins will be pardoned when you pray" (28:2).

If anyone suffered a grave injustice,
it was Jesus on the cross.
Remember what he said on the cross:
"Father, forgive them;
for they do not know
what they are doing" (Luke 23:34)
And remember the Our Father,
the prayer that Jesus taught us:
"Forgive us our trespasses
as we forgive those who trespass against us."

---

[26] Michael R. Kent, *Bringing the Word to Life (Year A)*, 111.

Wednesday

Deuteronomy 4:1,5–9
Matthew 5:17–19

The Path of Salvation

What we hear Jesus say today is pretty startling.
Even what he says to reassure us can be puzzling
in the light of some of his later actions.
"Do not think," he says, "that I have come
to abolish the law or the prophets;
I have come not to abolish but to fulfill.
For truly I tell you, until heaven and earth pass away,
not one letter, not one stroke of a letter,
will pass from the law,
until all is accomplished" (5:17–18).

But don't we see him, in practice,
bypassing "the Jewish law as the path of salvation"?
Don't we see him flouting "the law
when he healed on the sabbath,"
when he "ate with people
who were ceremonially unclean?"[27]
When the Pharisees see his disciples picking
heads of grain and eating them on the Sabbath,
they complain to Jesus and Jesus answers:
"Have you not read what David did
when he and his companions were hungry?
He entered the house of God
and ate the bread of the Presence,
which it was not lawful for him or his companions to eat,
but only for the priests" (Matthew 12:3–4).

---

[27] William Neil/Stephen Travis, *More Difficult Sayings of Jesus*, 65.

In the Light of the Lord

So what's the point of his saying that he didn't come
to abolish the law and the prophets but to fulfill them?
The likely answer is in the word "fulfill."
First of all, he says he came to fulfill
both the law and the prophets.
Prophecies are fulfilled,
but laws, we say, are obeyed, not fulfilled.
So if you say you're going to fulfill a law,
then you're seeing it as a kind of prophecy.
And, in fact, this is what Matthew does.
Later he will have Jesus say:
"For all the prophets and the law prophesied
until John [the Baptist] came" (11:13).
"Like the prophets, the Law pointed ahead
to Jesus the Messiah,"[28] to his mission, to his action,
to his teaching. "His teaching goes beyond the law,
yet the law was pointing in the same direction."[29]

Jesus, not the Law, is now the path to salvation.
The word "path" is the key to understanding
what this is all about. As the psalmist says,
"You will show me the path to life,
abounding joy in your presence . . ." (16:11).
In this psalm, Psalm 16, the word "path" is singular.
But when the verse is used in the Acts of the Apostles
and applied to Jesus, the word is said in the plural.
"You have made known to me the paths of life;
you will fill me with joy in your presence" (2:28).
Why plural? Because the words of Jesus
have become for us the paths of life.
The words of Jesus fulfill the law and the prophets.

[28]*Matthew*, 46.
[29]*More Difficult Sayings of Jesus*, 67.

In the Light of the Lord

Thursday

Jeremiah 7:23–28
Luke 11:14–23

Sins of the Spirit

Yesterday, in the first reading from Deuteronomy,
we heard Moses say:
"[W]hat other great nation has statutes and ordinances
as just as this entire law
that I am setting before you today?" (4:8)
And today, in Jeremiah: "This is the nation
that did not obey the voice of the LORD their God,
and did not accept discipline;
[faithfulness] has perished;
it is cut off from their lips" (7:28).

In the Hebrew language, according to scholars,
the word "faithfulness" implies:
"be what you are supposed to be.
It means consistency, fidelity."[30]

Opposed to it, therefore, is: Be what you are not.
Wear the mask of the person you pretend to be.
The shedding of the mask: that was the primary point
of Jesus' teaching against the Pharisees.
He called them hypocrites.
The word "hypocrite" means actor,
and an actor in Jesus' time wore a mask
that depicted the role he was playing.
It was Jesus seeing through their masks

---

[30]Carroll Stuhlmueller, *Biblical Meditations for Lent*, 45.

In the Light of the Lord

that angered the Pharisees.
Jesus was much more concerned
with sins of the spirit than sins of the flesh.
In terms of sins of the flesh,
the Pharisees were virtuous.
But wearing a mask is a sin of the spirit;
it's much more dangerous
"because it strikes at the vitals of the soul."[31]

So the Pharisees reach for a weapon of retaliation.
Slander is their weapon:
"It is by Beelzebul, the prince of devils,
that he casts out devils." Jesus responds:
"Every kingdom divided against itself cannot stand."
They are divided: their outer and their inner selves.
In the kingdom of God, there is a correspondence
between the outer and inner selves.
It is, in effect, the correspondence
between ourselves and Jesus.
As Jesus says: "Whoever is not with me
is against me" (Luke 11:23).

---

[31] See John A. Sanford, *The Kingdom Within*, 95–97.

Friday

Hosea 14:2–10
Mark 12:28–34

The Mind of Christ

According to the prophet Hosea,
Israel has fallen into idolatry.
How? By forming alliances with Assyria,
by trusting in their armed forces,
by saying 'Our God' to the work of their hands.
And so Hosea urges Israel to return to the Lord.
The Lord says: "I will heal their disloyalty,
I will love them freely" (14:4).

"Fill our hearts with your love,"
as we pray in the opening prayer.

"[T]he Lord our God is the one Lord,"
Jesus declares in the gospel,
citing the first of all the commandments.
"[Y]ou must love the Lord your God with all your heart,
with all your soul, with all your mind
and with all your strength" (Mark 12:29–30 NJB).

With all your *mind*. This phrase is not included
in Deuteronomy's account of the first commandment.
" . . . with all your heart, and with all your soul,
and with all your strength" (6:5),
but nothing is said about the mind.
Why is it added? What does it mean?

To love with all your mind
is to love with the mind of Christ.
As Saint Paul says: "Let the same mind
be in you that was in Christ Jesus" (Philippians 2:5).
Christ's mind: he had a mind to humble himself,
to give himself completely to God's purpose.
To love with all your mind
is to love God as Christ loved.
And the second command is like the first:
"You shall love your neighbor as yourself" (Mark 12:31).
Yes, we must have a mind for our neighbor too.

If we go along with this explanation
and if Jesus gives his approval,
he will say to us as he said to the scribe:
"You are not far from the kingdom of God" (12:34).

Saturday

Hosea 6:1–6
Luke 18:9–14

The Love That God Desires

Here we are at the end of the third week of Lent,
and tomorrow is Laetare Sunday,
which signals the joy toward which
the second phase of Lent is heading.
Today's opening prayer puts it very clearly:
"Lord, make this Lenten observance
of the suffering, death, and resurrection of Christ
bring us to the full joy of Easter."

In a way it echoes the people's prayer
in today's first reading from Hosea:
"Come, let us return to the LORD . . .
After two days he will revive us;
on the third day he will raise us up,
that we may live before him" (6:1–2).
This theme of salvation on the third day comes up
more than once in the Old Testament.[32]
Jesus brings it to absolute fulfillment
by rising from the dead "on the third day."

But the people's prayer, surprisingly, is not sincere.
"What shall I do with you, O Ephraim?
What shall I do with you, O Judah?" says the Lord.

---

[32] See *Biblical Meditations for Lent,* 49. (Other texts: Gn 42:18; Ex 19:10–11; Jos 3:2; Jon 2:1; Ezr 8:15; Est 5:1)

Both the northern country (Ephraim)
and the southern (Judah) have proved faithless
and their repentance is shallow and insincere.
"Your [piety] is like a morning cloud," the Lord says,
"like the dew that goes away early" (6:4).

What about the piety of the Pharisee,
as described in today's gospel?
His piety is also like a morning cloud,
and it is so packed with pride
that it will evaporate like dew.
He believes in his own righteousness,
he places all his trust in it.
Self-righteousness is the worst kind of sin
because it blinds one to the fact
that everything is a gift;
and it exempts one from the commandment,
"Love your neighbor as yourself,"
since everyone else is despised.
But if we don't love our neighbor,
how can we say we love God?

The tax collector, on the other hand,
admits all the wrongs he has done
and begs of God: "[B]e merciful to me, a sinner!" (18:13).
He stands before God, though at a distance,
not even raising his head,
but trusting in God's infinite mercy.
He recognizes fully the truth
that we heard in the first reading:
"For I desire steadfast love, not sacrifice . . ." (6:6)

As we enter this second phase of Lent,
let us sincerely acknowledge our failings

and trust in God's mercy and love
and love one another with the love that God desires.

Monday

Isaiah 65:17–21
John 4:43–54

Signs of New Life

Today we enter into the second phase of Lent.
In this phase, the gospel for each weekday Mass,
beginning with today's, is taken from Saint John.
Except for today, we'll be hearing, day after day,
about the mounting hostility toward Jesus
that climaxes in his suffering and death.

But today's gospel picks up on yesterday's theme,
sounding the joyful note of Laetare Sunday
that finds its full expression on Easter Sunday.
A royal official begs Jesus to come down
and restore health to his son, who is near death.
Jesus assures him, "[Y]our son will live" (4:50).
The father puts his trust in Jesus' word
and starts for home, and on his way there
he receives the good news that his son is going to live.

Jesus, the Son of God, is also near death.
Foreseeing the resurrection, we can say to the Father,
"Your Son will live."
Indeed, this is one way of expressing
our faith and trust and love for God.
"Your Son will live."

When Jesus said that and made it happen,
John writes that it was the second sign
that Jesus performed
on returning from Judea to Galilee.
The first sign was his changing water to wine
at the wedding in Cana.
These are signs that point to the new life
and to the new creation.
"[Look]," the Lord says in Isaiah, "I am about to create
new heavens and a new earth."
The pain and suffering of the past
"shall not be remembered or come to mind."
Instead, "be glad and rejoice forever
in what I am creating . . ." (65:17–18)

Thanks be to God.

Tuesday

Ezekiel 47:1–9, 12
John 5:1–3, 5–16

Rivers of Living Water

John in his gospel has Jesus perform seven signs.
By signs he means the wondrous deeds of Jesus.
In today's gospel we are given the third sign,
the healing of the paralytic
at the pool called Bethesda,
located near the Sheep Gate in Jerusalem.
The pool had five porticoes,
five walkways with columns supporting a roof.
(Excavations in Jerusalem have uncovered such a pool.)
The five porticoes were crowded with sick people,
with the lame, the blind, the crippled.
But Jesus healed only one,
one who had been sick for thirty-eight years.
Why didn't he heal all the others?
The fact that he didn't would seem to indicate
that physical healing was not Jesus' primary purpose.

"I am casting out demons
and performing cures today and tomorrow,"
Jesus said on another occasion,
"and on the third day
I [accomplish my purpose]" (Luke 13:32).
His "purpose" is not physical healings,
but healings do indeed point to his purpose.
On the third day he will rise from the dead,

and out of his heart will flow
"rivers of living water" (John 7:38).

Out of the temple, we hear in the first reading,
a river flows, giving life to trees on its banks
and to every sort of living creature,
"Wherever the river goes, . . .
there will be many fish,
once these waters reach there.
It will become fresh;
and everything will live . . ." (Ezekiel 47:9).

Christ is the new temple: "Destroy this temple,
and in three days I will raise it up" (John 2:19).
And the rivers of living water flowing from his heart
gives life to us all.

This is why he came.

Wednesday

Isaiah 49:8–15
John 5:17–30

Compassion Now and Always

In yesterday's gospel we heard how Jesus went one day
to the sheep pool in Jerusalem and cured a paralytic.
And that day was a Sabbath.
The Pharisees were outraged
and they began to persecute him.
And as we heard today
they were determined to kill him,
not only because he broke the Sabbath
but because he called God his father,
thereby making himself God's equal.
"My Father is still working," he said,
"and I also am working" (John 5:17).

Jesus seems to be saying, "My Father
rested on the Sabbath from the creating of things,
but his compassion for created things never rested.
His compassion is always at work, and so is mine."
But the Pharisees are saying, in effect:
Even compassion must stop on the Sabbath.

There are those who think that God's compassion
stops working not just on the Sabbath
but at a time when we most need it.
"The LORD has forsaken me,
my Lord has forgotten me" (Isaiah 49:14).

In the Light of the Lord

Words such as these, which we hear
in the first reading from the prophet Isaiah,
may well come from someone who has lost everything,
someone who has been violated,
someone who's been made to undergo great suffering.

But God powerfully responds to such words:
"Can a mother forget her nursing child,
or show no compassion for the child of her womb?
Even [she] may forget,
yet I will not forget you" (Isaiah 49:15).
God's compassion never forsakes us.
God's love never fails us.
A belief we need to deepen and hold on to
so it will always be with us,
especially when things are most difficult,
as it was for Jesus when he hung on the cross.

Thursday   *Exodus 32:7–14*
                                John 5:31–47

The Testimony of Good Works

Sometimes people on trial
will testify on their own behalf,
but their testimony is not as convincing
as that of others testifying for them.
Jesus says as much in the opening lines of the gospel:
"If I testify about myself,
my testimony is not true" (5:31).

In the first reading Moses testifies
on behalf of the people.
The Lord says to Moses:
"Go down at once! Your people,
whom you brought up out of the land of Egypt,
have acted perversely" (32:7).
Moses says in effect, Did you say my people?
They're *your* people, Lord. "[W]hy does your wrath
burn hot against your people?" (32:11)
And he reminds the Lord
of all he had done for his people
and all he promised to do, and the Lord relents.
Moses says, in effect, what we repeat
in the responsorial psalm:
"Lord, remember us, for the love you bear your people."

Jesus brings up more than one witness on his behalf.
The first is John the Baptist,
"a burning and shining lamp,"
in whose light, Jesus tells his accusers,
"you were willing to rejoice for a while" (John 5:35).

But Jesus claims to have testimony
greater than John's.
This greater testimony, he says, are "the works
that the Father has given me to complete" (5:36).
Father Ted Gabrielli, the pastor of a parish
in the poorest part of East Los Angeles,
once spoke about works.
Eleven gangs permeate his parish area,
and there are hundreds of homeless people,
and many of them spend the night in the church.
One member of a gang named Speedy
used to pester the homeless,
but one day Father Gabrielli found him badly beaten up.
He convinced him to come with him
to work in the parish,
and Speedy soon began helping
and feeding the homeless.
One day he went with Father Gabrielli to another church,
but there were no homeless there,
and he couldn't believe it was a Catholic Church.
Because he couldn't see any works,
it wasn't Catholic in his eyes.

Works are indeed strong testimony. As Jesus says,
"[T]he very works that I am doing testify on my behalf
that the Father has sent me" (5:36).
Good works are fueled by love,
and the reason his accusers refuse

to accept his works as testimony is because,
as Jesus says, they "do not have the love of God"
in their hearts (5:42).

In the light of this testimony, we pray again
what we prayed in the opening prayer:
"May the love within us be seen in what we do
and lead us to the joy of Easter."

Friday

Wisdom 2:1, 12–22
John 7:1–2, 10, 25–30

Who Do People Say That I Am

The Jewish feast of Tabernacles occurred
at the end of September and the beginning of October.
It was one of the obligatory festivals
for every adult male within fifteen miles of Jerusalem.
But devout Jews from far beyond came to it.[33]
Jesus' brothers went to it, and in a couple of verses
omitted in today's reading, they urged Jesus to go too,
so that people could see the works that he was doing.
But "not even his brothers," we're told,
"believed in him" (7:5)
Jesus declined to go: "My time has not yet come," he said.
However, as we heard in today's reading,
once his brothers had gone up to the feast,
he decided to go, "but as it were in secret" (7:6, 10).

And yet, in the temple precincts,
he began speaking in public.
Some of the people who heard him were puzzled.
"Why don't the authorities arrest him?"
"Maybe they've decided he is the Messiah."
"But he can't be, we know where this man is from."
This is the very opposite of popular belief:
the Messiah was supposed to just appear,
he would burst upon the scene mysteriously.

---

[33] See Barclay, *The Gospel of John*, vol. 1, 231.

In the Light of the Lord

No mystery, though, about where Jesus came from.
To which Jesus answers: So "You know me,
and you know where I am from.
I have not come on my own.
But the one who sent me is true,
and you do not know him.
I know him, because I am from him,
and he sent me" (7:28–29).

The people take those words as blasphemy.
And they react somewhat like the "wicked"
in today's first reading from the Book of Wisdom:
He "boasts that God is his father . . .
Let us condemn him to a shameful death" (2:16, 20).

The choice the people faced two thousand years ago
is, in a sense, still before us.
"Who do people say that I am?" (Mark 8:27)
Many Jews today, unlike the Pharisees, see Jesus
as an "admirable Jew," but not the Son of God.
Muslims recognize him as a great prophet
and revere him as Jesus, the son of Mary,
the only woman mentioned by name in the Koran.
We, of course, recognize him
not just as son of Mary, but as Son of God.
As Pope John Paul said:
"Christ is absolutely original and absolutely unique.
If he were only a wise man like Socrates,
if he were a prophet like Muhammad,
if he were enlightened like the Buddha,
without doubt he would not be what he is."[34]

---

[34] See *Newsweek*, March 27, 2000.

What we say to the Father in the opening prayer
we might well say now to Christ:
"May we reach out with joy to grasp your hand
and walk more readily in your ways."

Saturday

Jeremiah 11:18–20
John 7:40–53

The Way and The Truth and The Life

In his trial before Pilate, Jesus said,
"For this I was born,
and for this I came into the world,
to testify to the truth.
Everyone who belongs
to the truth listens to my voice."
Pilate said to him, "What is truth?" (John 18:37–38)
In today's gospel, "truth and untruth are in conflict.
The truth, whenever it is declared,
is countered with a generalization,"[35]
such as the ones we heard:
"Has any one of the authorities . . . believed in him?"
or, "This crowd, which does not know
the law, is accursed," and finally,
"[N]o prophet is to arise from Galilee" (John 7:48, 52).

---

[35] *O God Why?*, 122.

In the Light of the Lord

That last generalization
calls to mind something that Nathanael,
before he became an apostle, said to Philip:
"Can anything good come out of Nazareth?"
"Come and see," Philip said.
Nathanael went and saw.
Jesus said of him: "Here is truly an Israelite
in whom there is no deceit."
"Where did you get to know me?" Nathanael asked.
"I saw you under the fig tree . . ."
"Rabbi," Nathanael answered, "you are the Son of God."
Nathanael came to know the truth about Jesus
because he realized that somehow Jesus knew him.
Much to his astonishment,
Jesus revealed him to himself (John 1:43–51).

In the first reading, Jeremiah,
persecuted by his own people, says of the Lord,
You are the "searcher of mind and heart" (11:20).
And in the responsorial psalm we said of God:
You are the "searcher of heart and mind" (7:9 REB).

Gladly then, let us open our minds and hearts
to the Lord Jesus Christ,
so that even as he searches our hearts and minds
and reveals us to ourselves,
he will, by that very fact, reveal himself to us.
That brings us to an answer of Pilate's question:
What is truth?
Jesus is the truth. As he himself said, "I am
the way, and the truth, and the life" (John 14:6).

Monday

Trust in the Lord

The experiences described in today's readings
are similar to experiences we have undergone
or at least can readily appreciate.
Like being falsely accused
and helpless to explain ourselves.
Such was the experience of Susanna
in the first reading.
Or being guilty and having one's guilt
paraded before the world.
Such was the experience
of the woman taken in adultery.
Both experiences are of the kind
that cause humiliation,
a humiliation multiplied in our own day
of media intrusiveness and even irresponsibility.

That was the case of Cardinal Bernardin
a few years ago.
Before any proof had surfaced,
the media accused him before the world.
A week or so later
the charges against him were dropped.
Cardinal Bernardin wrote these words
in Chicago's archdiocesan newspaper:

"While I have not personally suffered
the horror of abuse,
I have felt the pain of being publicly humiliated.
In that sense, I am a victim who has survived.
I now have an even greater sensitivity to others
who have been victimized,
either by sexual abuse itself or by false accusation."

The key to survival is trust in the Lord.
Susanna, condemned to die, cries out to the Lord
and the Lord hears her prayer.
He stirs up the holy spirit of a young boy named Daniel,
and Daniel saves her. Blessed be God, the people cry,
the God "who saves those who hope in him" (Daniel 13:60).

Jesus, in the gospel, is like a new Daniel
with regard to the woman taken in adultery.
Her accusers could care less about her.
They're out to trap Jesus.
He was always befriending sinners,
even sitting down at table with them.
But here we have a clear case
of violation of Mosaic law
until Jesus dares to disown it.
"Let anyone among you who is without sin
be the first to throw a stone at her" (John 8:7).
It's not that he's soft on sin.
Go, he tells her, and sin no more.
But the sin of the accusers
is greater than the woman's,
the sin of self-righteousness, complacency,
readiness to use the law to condemn another
while confirming oneself in blindness of heart.

When we come before the Lord,
do we come telling the sins of others, or our sins?
If we want to experience God's mercy,
it had better be our sins.
There's a prayer of Blessed Peter Faber
with which we might aptly conclude:

I beg of you, my Lord,
to remove anything that separates
me from you, and you from me.

Remove anything that makes me unworthy
of your sight, your control, your reprehension;
of your speech and conversation,
of your benevolence and love.

Cast from me every evil
that stands in the way of my seeing you,
hearing, tasting, savoring, and touching you;
fearing and being mindful of you;
knowing, trusting, loving, and possessing you;
being conscious of your presence
and, as far as may be, enjoying you.

This is what I ask for myself
and earnestly desire from you. Amen.[36]

---

[36] *Hearts on Fire*, 25.

Tuesday

Numbers 21:4–9
John 8:21–30

The Sign of the Cross

The sign of the cross comes up in both readings today,
but in very symbolic terms,
and not easily comprehended.
Jesus says in the gospel,
"When you have lifted up the Son of Man,
then you will realize that I am he,
and that I do nothing on my own,
but I speak these things as the Father instructed me" (8:28).
Earlier, when he was talking to Nicodemus,
he was more specific about that lifting up.
"[J]ust as Moses lifted up the serpent in the wilderness,
so must the Son of Man be lifted up,
that whoever believes in him
may have eternal life" (John 3:14–15).

This refers, of course, to what we hear
in the first reading.
Moses, in accord with what the Lord had told him,
"made a serpent of bronze, and put it upon a pole;
and whenever a serpent bit someone,
that person would look at the serpent of bronze
and live" (21:9).
That bronze serpent was evidently highly prized,
because it showed up years later
in the temple of Jerusalem.

But King Hezekiah, who "pleased the Lord,"
"smashed the bronze serpent,"
we read in the second book of Kings,
"because up to that time the Israelites
were burning incense to it" (2 Kings 18:3–4).
I suppose that means that they were worshipping it.

Well, the cross is certainly not worshipped,
but it is highly revered. It is, of course, a sign.
It tells us that Jesus died once and for all,
it tells us that "God so loved the world
that he gave his only Son" (John 3:16).

As we gaze at Jesus on the cross,
we might well pray:
Soul of Christ, sanctify me.
Body of Christ, save me.
Blood of Christ, inebriate me.
Water from the side of Christ, wash me.
Passion of Christ, strengthen me.
O good Jesus, hear me.

Wednesday   *Daniel 3:14–20, 91–92, 95*
                                 John 8:31–42

The Truth of the Matter

In both readings we hear the Jews of different times
claiming to be children of the one true God.
In the first reading, from the Book of Daniel,
the three young Jews say they will die
for what they believe in.
In the gospel the Jews say they will kill for it.

At least this is what Jesus says of them:
"[Y]ou look for an opportunity to kill me,
because there is no place in you for my word" (John 8:37).

But who are the Jews to whom Jesus is speaking?
There's something more than a little confusing
in the gospel which you may or may not have noticed.
The first line of today's gospel has Jesus speaking
"to the Jews who believed in him,"
and he tells them: "If you continue in my word,
you are truly my disciples;
and you will know the truth,
and the truth will make you free" (8:31–32)
And they answer: "We are descendants of Abraham
and have never been slaves to anyone.
What do you mean by saying, 'You will be made free'?"
And Jesus says in response:
"Very truly, I tell you,

everyone who commits sin is a slave of sin . . .
I know that you are descendants of Abraham;
yet you look for an opportunity to kill me . . ." (8:33, 34, 37)

Is he still speaking to those Jews who believed in him?
If he is, why is he saying, You are trying to kill me?
According to *The New Jerome Biblical Commentary*,
when the evangelist refers to the Jews
who believed in Jesus, he is "thinking of
the Jewish Christians in his own time
faced with the choice of remaining Jesus' disciples
or abandoning their loyalty as 'disciples of Moses' . . .
As the dialogue progresses, these 'Christian Jews'
are merged with 'the Jews'
who are actively seeking Jesus' life' . . ."[37]

But to those of us today who believe in Jesus,
we can take those words of his to heart:
"If you continue in my word,
you are truly my disciples,
and you will know the truth,
and the truth will make you free" (8:31–32).

---

[37] *The New Jerome Biblical Commentary*, 966, #120.

Thursday   *Genesis 17:3–9*
                                              John 8:51–59

The Preeminence of Christ

The readings today describe a great arc of time,
reaching at both ends into eternity.
The promises made to Abraham reach forward
into our own time and beyond:
"[Y]ou will become the father
of many nations" (17:4 NJB).
The name *Abraham* means "The father is exalted."
I thought *father* would refer to Abraham,
but commentators say no, *father* is God—
God is exalted in Abraham and all his descendants—
not just of one nation, of one people:
no, he is to be the father of *many* nations.

In the gospel, Jesus solemnly declares:
"[B]efore Abraham was, I am" (8:58).
Jesus reaches into the past
beyond Abraham into eternity.
I AM. Another powerful name for God,
the *most* powerful: I am who am—
who is and who always will be—
the beginning and the end—
the source of all life and love.
Jesus is sent by the Father into the time of the gospel.
As Jesus says to the Pharisees:
"Your father Abraham rejoiced . . . that he would see my Day;
he saw it and was glad" (8:56 NJB).

In the Light of the Lord

It is as if Abraham saw "the whole history
of his descendants in a vision.
Jesus, therefore, is the true fulfillment
of their history"[38]—a history that began
with the promise of Abraham
and extends into our own day.

Which brings to mind that great passage
from Paul's letter to the Colossians,
thought to be an early Christian hymn
about the preeminence of Christ:
"He is the image of the invisible God,
the firstborn of all creation;
for in him all things in heaven and on earth
were created, things visible and invisible . . . ;
all things have been created through him
and for him.
He himself is before all things,
and in him all things hold together.
He is the head of the body, the church;
he is the beginning, the firstborn from the dead,
so that he might come to have first place in everything.
For in him all the fullness of God was pleased to dwell,
and through him God was pleased to reconcile to himself
all things, whether on earth or in heaven,
by making peace through the blood of his cross" (1:15–20).

---

[38]James McPolin, S.J., *John,* 132.

Friday

Jeremiah 20:10–13
John 10:31–42

Throwing Stones

This is the last Friday before Good Friday,
and the readings of the day foreshadow
what we know will happen on Good Friday.
Jesus more than once denounces the Pharisees
for their attitude and conduct. On one occasion
he tells them what "the wisdom of God" said:
" 'I will send them prophets and apostles,
some of whom they will kill and persecute,'
so that this generation may be charged
with the blood of all the prophets shed
since the foundation of the world . . ." (Luke 11:49–50).

In the first reading we hear the prophet Jeremiah
declare how his friends had become his enemies.
"Perhaps he can be enticed," they said;
"and we can prevail against him,
and take our revenge on him" (20:10).
We don't know how he actually died,
but there is a legend, not history but a legend,
that he was stoned to death by the Jews in Egypt.[39]

Which resonates with what we hear in today's gospel.
When the Jews picked up rocks to stone him,

---

[39]See McKenzie, *Dictionary of the Bible*, 421.

Jesus says to them: "I have shown you
many good works from the Father.
For which of these are you going to stone me?" (10:31)

Do we throw stones at others?
Stones of rash judgment,
of self-righteousness, of condemnation?
Or are stones thrown at us?
If the former, then during these last days of Lent
let us drop the stones and reach out for reconciliation.
If the latter, if stones are thrown at us,
then let us do as we say in the responsorial psalm:
"In my distress I called upon the LORD;"
I called to him for help;
"and my cry . . . reached his ears" (Psalm 18:6).

"I love you, O LORD, my strength,
The LORD is my rock, my fortress, and my deliverer."

Saturday   *Ezekiel 37:21–28*
                                               John 11:45–56

God's People

In both readings
there is the vision of one nation, secure and undivided,
but how different the ways and means!
In the first reading,
God promises through the prophet Ezekiel
to bring together the two kingdoms, Israel and Judah,
to bring the scattered Jews into one nation
and to cleanse them of all their sins and infidelities
so that they may be his people and he may be their God.

In the gospel, a few centuries later,
the Jews are still one nation
but they are under Roman jurisdiction
and they are afraid that if Jesus rises in power
he will be a threat to their national security.
Many who witnessed the raising of Lazarus
believed in Jesus,
but others reported to the Pharisees what he had done,
and the Pharisees got together with the chief priests,
who were all Sadducees, in a meeting of the Sanhedrin.
"What are we to do?" they said (11:47).
"You know nothing at all" said Caiphas the high priest.
"You do not understand that it is better for you
to have one man die for the people
than to have the whole nation destroyed" (11:49–50).

Well, what Caiphas was saying is a classic example
of dramatic irony. Dramatic irony occurs
when a character in a play doesn't realize
the full significance of what he's saying.[40]
As John explains it, Caiphas is actually prophesying
that Jesus would die for the nation,
"and not for the nation only, but to gather into one
the dispersed children of God" (11:52).
We have an echo here of what God said through Ezekiel:
"[T]hey will be my people,
and I shall be their God" (37:23 NJB).

We do well to enter Holy Week with this in mind.
As we say in the opening prayer:
"God our Father, you always work to save us."
God works to save us through his Son Jesus Christ.
"And now we rejoice," we said, "in [your] great love."
"No one has greater love than this,
to lay down one's life for one's friends" (John 15:13).
Love such as this makes God our God,
and makes us God's people.

---

[40]See Barclay, *The Gospel of John,* vol. 2, 105.

Monday

Isaiah 42:1–7
John 12:1–11

The Fragrance of the Oil

Today's reading from Isaiah is the first
of the four songs of the Suffering Servant.
Tomorrow we hear the second song,
and on Wednesday the third (the third
having been already heard on Passion Sunday),
and the fourth demands our attention on Good Friday.
How readily we see Jesus in the Suffering Servant
as Isaiah describes him in the four songs.
As we hear today:
"Here is my servant, whom I uphold,
my chosen, in whom my soul delights" (42:1).
These words, as you may recall,
resonate with those heard at Jesus' baptism:
"This is my beloved Son,
with whom I take delight" (Matthew 3:17 REB).

"I am the LORD," we hear him say in Isaiah;
"I have called you in righteousness,
I have taken you by the hand and kept you;
I have given you as a covenant of the people,
a light to the nations . . ." (42:6).

It is truly remarkable how this song
and the other three foreshadow who Jesus is,
what he does and what is done to him.

Today's gospel is also a foreshadowing,
a foreshadowing of the death and burial
and even the resurrection of Jesus.
Mary, the sister of Lazarus
whom Jesus had raised from the dead,
anoints the feet of Jesus
with a "costly perfume,"
made from the oil of a plant called nard,
and "the house was filled
with the fragrance of the perfume" (12:3).
When Judas blasts her for wasting all that money,
Jesus says, "Leave her alone.
She bought it so that she might keep it
for the day of my burial" (12:7).
And the house, we heard, was filled
with the fragrance of the oil.
That fragrance "heralds Jesus' resurrection."[41]

Once again we pray:
Soul of Christ, sanctify me.
Body of Christ, save me.
Blood of Christ, inebriate me.
Passion of Christ, strengthen me.
O good Jesus, hear me.

---

[41] Lee & Honner, *Wisdom and Demons*, 92.

Tuesday

Isaiah 49:1–6
John 13:21–33, 36–38

The Giving of a Name

Isaiah's songs of the Suffering Servant
are sung now *of* Jesus and *by* Jesus.
From the second song, today's first reading,
we can hear Jesus say:
"The LORD called me before I was born,
while I was in my mother's womb he named me" (49:1).
It's not that God gave him the name of Jesus.
"Jesus," as we know, was a common Hebrew name,
meaning "God saves."
"To give him his name" is a way of saying
that God calls him from birth to be and to do,
as no other shall be or do.
"I will give you as a light to the nations," God says,
"that my salvation may reach
to the end of the earth" (49:6).

How will Jesus be and do all this?
By living and dying for us all.
He says to his apostles what he once said to the Jews:
"Where I am going, you cannot come."
"Where are you going?" Simon Peter asks.
"Where I am going, you cannot follow me now,
but you will follow afterward" (John 13:36).

Follow him, yes, follow him into death;
but Jesus meant more:
follow him into the mystery of God.
He knew that he came from God
and that he was going back to God (John 13:3),
a movement that describes the great arc of his life,
a movement that begins
with God calling him from birth
and giving him his name;
and ends with God giving him the name
that is above every other name:
Jesus is the Lord (Philippians 2:9,11).

In the words of the Suffering Servant,
we say *with* Jesus and *for* Jesus:
"I am honored in the sight of the Lord,
and my God has become my strength!" (Isaiah 49:5).

And in the words of the responsorial psalm:
"For you are my hope, O Lord;
my trust, O God, from my youth.
On you I depend from birth;
from my mother's womb you are my strength" (Psalm 71:5).

Wednesday

Isaiah 50:4–9
Matthew 26:14–25

Betrayal

Spy Wednesday. This name is not as common
as Holy Thursday or Good Friday.
But today has been called Spy Wednesday
because it commemorates what Judas said and did.

When Jesus chose Judas as one of the Twelve,
he certainly didn't choose him with betrayal in mind.
To be betrayed by someone you know and love:
that was no doubt one of the hardest things
that Jesus had to bear in his Passion.
I've heard it said that "betrayal is only possible
where love has been given."[42]

It is while he's reclining at table with the Twelve
that Jesus says, "One of you is to betray me."
One after another the apostles begin to say,
"Surely it is not I, Lord."
All but one address him with the title of "Lord," Kyrie.
Judas betrays himself when he uses the title "Rabbi."
"Surely [it is] not I, Rabbi."
"You have said so" (26:21–25).
This is what Jesus says in reply—"an ambiguous phrase
which throws the responsibility for the question
back on the questioner: 'You said it, not I.' "[43]

---

[42]Robert Johann, *Building the Human*, 150.
[43]Meier, *Matthew*, 317.

This incident follows shortly after that time
when Jesus was reclining at table
in the house of Simon the leper
and a woman came up to him with an alabaster jar
of costly perfumed oil and poured it on his head.
When the disciples saw this, they were indignant
and said, "Why this waste?
For this ointment could have been sold for a large sum,
and the money given to the poor" (26:6–9).
Judas was especially indignant.
He no longer believed in Jesus;
Jesus is not the kind of leader he wanted him to be.
So now after the incident at the Last Supper
he goes to the chief priests
and sells him for thirty pieces of silver.
Somewhat less, I would imagine,
than he would have got for the costly perfumed oil.
But when he sees what happens,
he deeply regrets the terrible thing he has done.

Jesus once said,
"What you did for the least of my brethren
you did also for me" (Matthew 25:40).
May our love for Jesus be such
that we will not betray him
by using other people for our own advantages
and dismissing them when they cease to be of use.

Holy Thursday

Exodus 12:1–8, 11–14
1 Corinthians 11:23–26
John 13:1–15

In the Upper Room

There's a story about a group of Chinese Christians
who invited an American biblical scholar
to come give them a workshop on Scripture.
In the course of the workshop,
the scholar asked the participants to select
the episode in the gospel that impressed them most.
To his surprise, these Chinese Christians
did not pick the Sermon on the Mount
or the crucifixion or the resurrection of Jesus.
They picked rather the story
of Jesus washing his disciples' feet.[44]

Surprising perhaps, but upon reflection
the episode is especially revelatory
of who Jesus is and what he came to do.
What inspires Jesus' action?
As John says in today's gospel,
knowing "that he had come from God
and was going to God" (13:3),
Jesus rises from the table.
Yes, because of that realization,
that he had come from God and was returning to God,
Jesus gets up to wash his disciples' feet.
The performance of that simple action

[44]Mark Link, S.J., *Vision 2000*, 110.

In the Light of the Lord

is meant to reveal why he had been sent
and how the apostles were to remember him.
"You call me Teacher and Lord—and you are right,
for that is what I am. So if I,
your Lord and Teacher, have washed your feet,
you also ought to wash one another's feet.
For I have set you an example,
that you also should do
as I have done to you" (13:13–15).
Jesus meant what he said,
Jesus meant what he did.
His disciples are to serve one another
because he came to serve.
They are to give of themselves
because he came to give.
They may not understand
the full meaning of his action now,
as he said to Peter, but they will when he goes
as far as his love will carry him—to the cross.

So too with the Eucharist.
It is only in the light of that love
that the Eucharist has any meaning at all.
The Eucharist reveals Christ's desire
to be with us always; this sacrament, we say,
makes him truly present. But when we say
it makes him present we haven't said it all.
What the Eucharist does is make Christ present
in the very act of giving,
in the very act of loving us "to the end" (13:1).
For as often as [we] eat this bread and drink this cup,
as we heard Paul say in the second reading,
"[we] proclaim the death of the Lord

until he comes" (1 Corinthians 11:26), i.e., we proclaim
his once-for-all self-giving on the cross.

When Pope John Paul was in the Holy Land
in the Jubilee Year, he was able to spend some time
in the Upper Room, the room of the Last Supper;
and he sent his Holy Thursday letter to priests,[45]
in which he said something that we all do well to hear.
"Two thousand years after the birth of Christ,"
he wrote, ". . . we especially need
to remember and ponder the truth
of what we might call his 'Eucharistic birth.'
The Upper Room is the place of this 'birth.'
Here began a new presence of Christ for the world,
a presence which constantly occurs
whenever the Eucharist is celebrated
and a priest lends his voice to Christ,
repeating the sacred words of institution.
This Eucharistic birth has accompanied
the two thousand years of the Church's history,
and it will do so until the end of time.
For us it is both a joy and a source of responsibility
to be so closely linked to this mystery.
Today we want to become
more deeply aware of his presence,
our hearts filled with wonder and gratitude,
and in this spirit to enter the Easter Triduum
of the Passion, Death and Resurrection of Jesus" (13).

"From the Upper Room," Pope John Paul concludes,
"I embrace you in the Eucharist.

---

[45]March 23, 2000.

May the image of Christ
surrounded by his own at the Last Supper
fill each of us with a vibrant sense
of [companionship] and communion" (15).
Amen.[46]

---

[46]Adapted, in part, from the author's *The Paths of Life*, Cycle B, 62–64.

In the Light of the Lord

Good Friday

Isaiah 52:13–53:12
Hebrews 4:14–16; 5:7–9
John 18:1–19:42

The Ultimate Epiphany

"They will look on the one
whom they have pierced" (John 19:37).
They looked on him then;
we look on him now.
Why? Because Jesus on the cross
is Jesus exposed to our view as never before.
A better way of saying this
is that Jesus on the cross
is Jesus in a supreme moment of revelation.
The cross is the ultimate epiphany.
It shows how far sin will go,
and how far love will go.
"[H]e was wounded for our transgressions,
crushed for our [sins]," we hear Isaiah say.
"Upon him was the punishment
that made us whole,
by his bruises we are healed" (53:5).

Sin rejects the love of God
that Jesus offers in his very person
and nails him to a cross;
but that rejection enables love
to be revealed at its most powerful.

"Not only is the cross the result of sin,
it is the event that heals sin.
The cross now cuts two ways.
It reveals [our] human resistance" to God's love
and God's persistence in breaking it down.[47]

"It is finished."
These are the last words, in John's account,
that Jesus speaks from the cross (19:30).
"It is finished," as if to say,
"The cross brings to completion
what I came to do:
to show that God is love
and love is stronger than death."[48]

As Julian of Norwich says:
" . . . the love that made him suffer all this—
it passes as far beyond all his pains
as heaven is above earth.
For the passion was a deed done in time
by the working of love;
but the love is without beginning,
and is, and ever shall be, without . . . end."[49]

[47]John Shea, *An Experience Named Spirit*, 199.
[48]Adapted from the author's *The Paths of Life*, Cycle B, 64–65.
[49]*The Showing of God's Love*, ch. XI.

Easter

Monday

Acts 2:14, 22–32
Matthew 28:8–15

Praise the Lord

Alleluia. This word means "Praise the Lord";
and after weeks of omission it comes up again
at the beginning of the Easter season.
As Saint Augustine said:
"We are Easter people and Alleluia is our song."
And we stand up for the Alleluia—
as a physical reminder of Resurrection.[1]

Know

In the first reading, we hear how Peter
stood up with the Eleven, raised his voice,
and addressed the people:
Listen to what I have to say.
And he tells them about Jesus the Nazarean,
"attested to you by God
with deeds of power, wonders and signs,
that God did through him among you,
as you yourselves know" (2:22).
And then he quotes Psalm 16 to them,
declaring that it is fulfilled in Jesus.
"God raised this man Jesus to life,
and of that we are all witnesses" (2:32 NJB).

In Psalm 16 is the great line:
"You will show me the path of life.

[1]*The Vatican II Weekday Missal*, 668.

In your presence there is fullness of joys" (16:11).
But Peter, using the Greek translation of the psalm,
changes the word "path" from singular to plural:
"You have made known to me the paths of life" (Acts 2:28).
Does this change make any difference?
I would say it relates to what Jesus said and did.
It reminds us that the Jesus who was raised in glory
is the same Jesus
who ate and drank with his disciples.
Like the marks of the Passion,
he carries with him all his human experiences,
carries them into his new life with God.
No wonder that the early Church
took such pains to remember and record them.
All these accounts of what Jesus said and did
can lead us to an ever deeper
and more loving relationship with him;
they can become for us "the paths of life."

In the Light of the Lord

Tuesday

Acts 2:36–41
John 20:11–18

The Risen Lord

The Peter we meet in today's first reading
is a very different Peter
from the one we encountered last week.
Last week we heard Jesus say
that Peter would deny him three times.
And indeed Peter gives in to fear.
But now, he is full of courage,
and he speaks out to all the Jews
about the gift of the Holy Spirit,
a gift that he himself has already received.

In the gospel, we meet Mary Magdalene,
and we see a very different Mary at the end
from the Mary we saw at the beginning.
At the beginning, she is still inconsolable,
weeping for one she so loved.
"Why are you weeping?" she hears someone say.
It's as if tears have blurred
the vision of her eyes of faith.
"The failure to see is overcome
only when Jesus calls her by name."
As Raymond Brown reminds us, the Good Shepherd
"calls by name the sheep that belong to him,
sheep that will not follow a stranger
'because they do not recognize

the voice of strangers'" (John 10:5).
Mary immediately recognizes Jesus
and "addresses him as Rabbouni,
an endearing term for Teacher."[2]

"Don't cling to me." Not: "Don't touch me."
He will tell the doubting Thomas to touch his wounds.
Why is he telling Mary not to cling to him?
One reason is that he is entrusting her
with a mission. "[G]o to my brothers and say to them,
'I am ascending to my Father and your Father,
to my God and your God'" (20:17).
Jesus, at the Last Supper, had said to his apostles:
"I shall no longer call you servants. . . ,
I call you friends" (John 15:15 NJB).
And now he calls them "brothers,"
because as he says, My Father is your Father.
The family of God has been created anew.

Mary Magdalene goes on her mission:
"I have seen the Lord!" (20:18)
"Jesus is now more than the 'Rabbouni'
whom she lovingly recognized
when he first called her name . . .
Magdalene is the first to proclaim *the risen Lord*." [3]
This she proclaims to the apostles,
and she proclaims it to us as well.
In the light of so bright a proclamation,
may we see Jesus more clearly,
love him more ardently,
and follow him more closely.

---

[2]Brown, *A Risen Christ in Eastertime*, 71-72.
[3]Brown, 73.

In the Light of the Lord

Wednesday

Acts 3:1–10
Luke 24:13–35

The Beautiful

The temple gate called "the Beautiful Gate"—
thought to be the gate
decorated with Corinthian bronze
that separated the court of women
from the court of Gentiles.
It was called "the Beautiful Gate" no doubt
because of what it looked like
in comparison to all the other gates;
but there's a new reason now: now it's beautiful
because of the beauty of the risen Christ.
"I have no silver or gold," Peter declares,
"but what I have I give you;
In the name of Jesus Christ of Nazareth,
[rise] up and walk" (Acts 3:6).
And the man crippled from birth rose up and walked.
That was indeed something beautiful to see.

Wherever Christ appeared,
wherever his presence and power made itself felt,
that place was rendered beautiful.
Today's gospel recalls for us one of many apparitions.
Christ had appeared in the garden, in the upper room,
behind locked doors, on the beach.
Now he appears on the road to Emmaus,
and, most significantly, in the breaking of the bread.

"Then," we read, "[the] eyes [of the two disciples]
were opened, and they recognized him" (24:31).
Yes, the eyes of the flesh were not enough;
it took the eyes of the soul,
the eyes of faith, to recognize him.

"I am with you always," Christ promised,
"to the end of [time]" (Matthew 28:20).
He is with us from moment to moment,
in the breaking of the bread—a moment made beautiful
by the presence and power of his love.
When we receive the sacrament of that love,
we share in love's presence and power.
Hopefully, we will feel it
from moment to moment in our lives.
Hopefully, we can make it felt
in all our words and actions,
so that they will be like gates for God's love,
and that would certainly make them beautiful.

Thursday

Acts 3:11–26
Luke 24:35–48

With the Eyes of the Soul

"This is the day the Lord has made:
let us rejoice and be glad."

Each day in Easter Week
celebrates Jesus' resurrection.
Each day's gospel recounts one of his appearances.
Today's appearance occurs very soon after yesterday's.
The two disciples who had been on the way to Emmaus
are returned to Jerusalem
and are telling the eleven apostles
what had happened when suddenly Jesus himself
is standing in their midst.
"Peace be with you," he says (24:36).
But the Eleven in their panic and fright
think they are seeing a ghost.
"Touch me and see," Jesus says,
"for a ghost does not have flesh and bones
as you see I have" (24:39).
And he does for them what he had done
for the two disciples on the way to Emmaus:
he opens their minds to the understanding
of the Scriptures: how "everything written about me
in the law of Moses, the prophets and psalms
must be fulfilled" (24:44).

Peter was impressed, to put it mildly.
When we meet him in the first reading
talking to the people in Solomon's portico,
he tells them that "all the prophets, . . .
from Samuel and those after him,
also predicted these days.
You are the descendants of the prophets
and of the covenant that God gave to your ancestors,
saying to Abraham, '[I]n your descendants
all the families of the earth
shall be blessed'" (3:24–25).
All the families of the earth—
that includes you and me.
We are among the blessed.
"Blessed are those who have not seen
and yet have come to believe" (John 20:29).
We have not seen Christ, as the apostles did,
with the eyes of the flesh.
But what really matters is to see Christ
with the eyes of the soul,
to recognize him in the breaking of the bread,
and to take him at his word
that he will be with us always,
all the days of our life.

Let us close with a prayer
(a prayer by Carlo Maria Martini, Cardinal of Milan):
"Lord Jesus, we ask you now
to help us to remain with you always,
to be close to you with all the ardor of our hearts,
to take up joyfully the mission you entrust to us,
and that is to continue your presence
and spread the good news of your Resurrection."[4]

---

[4]*Hearts on Fire*, 82.

In the Light of the Lord

Friday

Acts 4:1–12
John 21:1–14

The Breaking of the Bread

Jesus said some great things
and he said some simple things.
But even the simple things have great connotations.
"Come, have breakfast," he said to his disciples
when they landed on shore.
That's certainly a simple saying, but it means a lot.
There are so many meals in the gospels!
Why?
Well, because meals are so natural,
so desirable, so communal.

Jesus often met with people at meals.
He often met with his disciples at meals.
Even as the risen Lord he met with them at meals.
Maybe I should say: especially as the risen Lord.
How very natural, how very desirable that was.
And they recognized him at the breaking of the bread.
As we hear today in the gospel,
"none of the disciples dared to ask him, 'Who are you?'
because they knew it was the Lord" (21:12).

The early Christians, we're told,
devoted themselves to meet every day
at the breaking of bread in their homes.
They gathered at a meal to be one with Christ
and with each other. And so do we.

Because we eat the one bread, Saint Paul says,
we are one body (1 Corinthians 10:17).
The Eucharist makes us one with the risen Lord
and with each other.
As Pope John Paul says in one of his encyclicals,
the Lord "unites us with himself and with one another
by a bond stronger than any natural union;
and thus united, he sends us into the whole world
to bear witness to God's love
through faith and works . . ."[5]

"This is the day the Lord has made;
let us rejoice and be glad," as we proceed now
with the celebration of the Eucharist.

---

[5]*Sollicitudo rei socialis*, no. 48.

In the Light of the Lord

Saturday

Not Seeing and Believing

Most manuscripts of Saint Mark's gospel
end with what we hear in today's gospel,
a brief account of a number of appearances
of the risen Jesus.
As noted in the *Vatican II Weekday Missal*,
it makes an excellent conclusion to the gospels
of this Easter Week. But scholars agree
that its "vocabulary and style indicate
that it was written by someone other than Mark."[6]
Mark's gospel, if you recall, ends with verse 8,
which states that the three women,
including Mary Magdalene, who entered the tomb
and were told by a young man to go and tell
the disciples that Jesus had been raised,
"went out and fled from the tomb"
and "said nothing to anyone, for they were afraid."

What were they afraid of?
Well, one thing they might have been afraid of
is that what they had heard was not true.

That keeps coming up; those who knew Jesus
do not believe that he was raised from the dead
until they see him with their own eyes.

---

[6]*The New American Bible*, footnote 16:9-20, 94.

Mary Magdalene went a second time to the tomb,
and this time she saw him with her own eyes,
and then, as we heard in today's gospel,
when she went and told his companions
"that he was alive and had been seen by her,
they would not believe it" (16:10–11). And later,
when the two disciples from Emmaus
returned and told the disciples what they had seen,
"they did not believe them" either (16:13).
And as we will hear in tomorrow's gospel,
Thomas wouldn't believe that Jesus was risen
because he wasn't there when Jesus appeared
to all the other disciples.

And yet, as we hear in the first reading,
two of those disciples, Peter and John,
go all around Jerusalem preaching the risen Jesus.
And when they are arrested, they tell the court:
"[W]e cannot keep from speaking
about what we have seen and heard" (4:20).
And the court can find no way to punish them,
"because of the people, for all of them
praised God for what had happened" (4:21).
So these people believed
even though they had not seen.
As the risen Jesus says to Thomas:
"Blessed are those who have not seen
and yet have come to believe" (John 20:29).

And this includes each and every one of us.
What really matters, as we've considered before,
is to see Christ with the eyes of the soul,
to recognize him in the breaking of the bread.

In the Light of the Lord

Monday

Acts 4:23–31
John 3:1–8

Water and Spirit

During this season when we celebrate the risen Jesus,
the Holy Spirit rises up in our minds and hearts.
This is inevitably so, because as John tells us
in a later chapter, until Jesus is glorified
the sending of the Spirit cannot take place (7:39).

As we hear in the first reading,
after Peter and John were released from prison
and returned to their people,
the place where they were gathered
shook as they prayed,
and they were filled with the Holy Spirit
and continued to speak the word of God
"with boldness" (4:31).

In the gospel, Jesus tells Nicodemus
"no one can enter the kingdom of God
without being born of water and Spirit" (3:5).
This is generally understood as a reference
to the sacrament of baptism,
"but that meaning is at most secondary.
Water in [John's] gospel is a symbol of the Spirit."[7]
As Jesus says on the last day
of the Feast of the Tabernacles,

---

[7]"*I Encountered God!*," 58.

"Let anyone who is thirsty come to me. . . and drink.
As the scripture has said,
'Out of the believer's heart
shall flow rivers of living water.'"
"Now he said this about the Spirit,"
John explains, "which believers in him
were to receive" (7:37–39).

God will not deny us his Spirit.
"Ask and you will receive," Jesus said,
"so that your joy may be complete" (John 16:24).
Only the Spirit can give fullness of joy.

In the Light of the Lord

Tuesday

Wind and Spirit

Have you ever seen a field of tall grass
rippling like the waves of a sea?
Obviously, the wind was blowing through it,
but you couldn't see the wind, only the effects of it.
This is very much like what Jesus tells Nicodemus
in today's gospel.
In both Hebrew and Greek the word for "wind" and "spirit"
is the same: *pneuma* in Greek, *rûah* in Hebrew.[8]
"The wind blows where it chooses,
and you hear the sound of it,
but you do not know
where it comes from or where it goes;
so it is with everyone who is born of the Spirit" (3:8).

But Nicodemus asks, "How can these things be?"
And Jesus says to him, "Are you a teacher of Israel
and yet you do not understand these things?"
I must say, I asked myself if I understood it.
Are these the words of Jesus
or of John the evangelist?
Actually, three times in his conversation
with Nicodemus, Jesus begins with the phrase,
"Very truly, I say to you";
and this phrase comes up not just in John's gospel

---

[8]*The New American Bible*, footnote 3:8, 149.

but in the synoptics as well, and some scholars say
that when that phrase is used,
we're hearing the words of Jesus.

There are a number of things in this world
that we often use without knowing how they work.
Whenever I use the Internet
I have no idea how it works,
but I'll search for this or that
and get all sorts of results.
We may not understand how and why the wind blows,
but we can see what it does.
So too with the Spirit.
We may not know how the Spirit works,
but we can see the effect of the Spirit
in human lives.[9]

Born from above, born of the Spirit.
Jesus declares that the one who believes
must undergo a spiritual rebirth,
must enter a new life,
which he himself calls "eternal life."
("Eternal" is a better word than "everlasting."
"The main idea behind eternal life
is not simply that of duration."
Eternal life is "the life of God."[10])

This is something we pray for in the opening prayer.
"All-powerful God, help us to proclaim
the power of the Lord's resurrection.
May we who accept this sign of the love of Christ
come to share the eternal life he reveals."

---

[9]Cf. Barclay, *John*, vol. 1, 131-132.
[10]Barclay, 128-129.

Wednesday   *Acts 5:17–26*
                                 John 3:16–21

New Life

The apostles were becoming very popular,
and the high priest and his party of Sadducees
got so jealous that they threw them in jail.
But there was no stopping them.
As we hear in the first reading,
an angel of the Lord unlocked the doors
and set the apostles free and told them
to take their place in the temple precincts
and to tell the people everything about this life.

What life is that?
Some translations add the word "new."
And the *Jerusalem Bible* capitalizes the word "Life."
Go and "tell the people all about this new Life" (5:20).
So what exactly did they tell the people?
All we know is that they went to the temple
and taught, but they could well have used
the very first sentence of the gospel:
"[G]od so loved the world that he gave his only Son,
so that everyone who believes in him
may not perish but may have eternal life" (3:16).

Eternal life. The very life of God himself.
These words tell us essential things about God.

God is love—"the mainspring of God's being is love."[11]
Everything begins with God, begins with love.
God sends his Son as the full expression of that love.

God so loved the world, not just this people
or that people, but the world, everybody.
As Saint Augustine puts it: "God loves each of us
as if there was only one of us to love."

Let each of us then love God
in his only Son, Jesus Christ.
To quote Saint Clare (from her third letter to Blessed Agnes):
May you "totally love Him
who gave Himself totally for your love."[12]
And she quotes him, saying, "Whoever loves me
will be loved by my Father,
and I too shall love him,
and we shall come to him
and make our dwelling place with him" (John 14:21, 23).

This sums up the "new life" the apostles preached,
to the people of their day there in the temple,
and to us today in this church.

[11]Cf. Barclay, *John*, vol. 1, 136-138.
[12]*Clare of Assisi: Early Documents*, 45.

Thursday

Acts 5:27–33
John 3:31–36

The Penetrating Light of Christ

Peter and the apostles are arrested again,
after they were caught preaching in the temple area,
preaching the "new life" that the angel,
who had freed them from prison, urged them to do.
They claim to be witnesses of the new life,
witnesses of the risen Jesus.
And as we hear them tell the Sanhedrin,
the holy Spirit is also a witness, "the holy Spirit
whom God has given to those who obey him" (5:32).

When the Sanhedrin hear this,
they are so infuriated that they want to kill them.
They thus bring judgment upon themselves.
This resonates with what John says in today's gospel:
"Whoever believes in the Son has eternal life;
whoever disobeys the Son will not see life,
but must endure God's wrath" (3:36).
Which is another way of saying,
they must endure God's judgment.
"And this is the judgment,"
as John said in yesterday's gospel,
"that the light has come into the world,
and people loved darkness rather than light
because their deeds were evil" (3:19).
The light that has come into the world is Christ.

Christ is "a penetrating light that provokes judgment"
by making apparent what we are, by bringing out
whatever is good in us, whatever is evil.[13]

Whatever is evil corresponds to disobedience.
That's why John said,
"[W]hoever disobeys the Son will not see life" (3:36).
That's why Peter said to the Sanhedrin,
God gives the Holy Spirit to those who obey him (5:32).

May our every word and action
give us the right to pray
that simple but important prayer:
Come, Holy Spirit!

[13]Raymond E. Brown, *The Gospel According to John*, vol. 29, 148.

Friday

Acts 5:34–42
John 6:1–15

For the Sake of the Name

In sign language the sign of Jesus is this:
the middle finger of one hand
touching the palm of the other,
and then the converse.
This sign of Jesus says immediately:
"the one who was crucified."
I venture to say it also connotes
"the one who rose from the dead,"
the Jesus who appears to the apostles
when Thomas is there with them and says to him:
"Put your finger here and see my hands" (John 20:27).
The one who was crucified for us
and for us rose from the the dead.
All that, at least, is contained in the name of Jesus.

I fix on this because, reflecting on today's scripture,
I keep coming back to the verse in the first reading
from the Acts of the Apostles:
As the apostles left the Sanhedrin,
"they rejoiced that they were considered worthy
to suffer dishonor for the sake of the name" (5:41).
For the sake of the name
of the one who died for us
and for us rose from the dead.

And to be allowed to suffer for that name
fills them with joy.

So we see that from the beginning of Christianity
there was joy in the midst of suffering
endured for the sake of the name.
Saints and martyrs often bring this to mind.
There were those twenty-six martyrs in Nagasaki,
some of them Jesuits, some of them Franciscans,
and when they were tied to a cross
they burst into song.
One of them, named Paul Miki, preached to the onlookers,
said that he was joyfully giving his life for Christ,
and then forgave his executioners.
Saint Ignatius, in the third week
of the Spiritual Exercises,
has one pray for the grace to imitate Christ
"in bearing all injuries and affronts."
But to bear them with joy? How can that be done?

The poet Gerard Manley Hopkins,
meditating on Our Lady's sorrow,
once wrote in his diary:
"Christ's joy in spite of sorrow.
Wish to enter into this."
Joy in spite of sorrow, joy in the midst of sorrow.
Not the feeling of joy: that is never in our power.
Rather, an essential joy rooted in the recognition
of who Christ is, who Christ is for us.
The name of Jesus says it all:
the name of the one who suffered and died for us
and for us rose from the dead.

Saint Peter, in his first letter, sums it up for us:
"Blessed be God the Father of our Lord Jesus Christ,
who in his great mercy
has given us a new birth into a living hope
through the resurrection
of Jesus Christ from the dead . . .
This is a great joy to you,
even though [for a little while]
you must bear all sorts of trials . . .
You have not seen him, yet you love him;
and still without seeing him you believe in him
and so are already filled with a joy so glorious
that it cannot be described . . ." (1:3, 6, 8 NJB).

Saturday

Acts 6:1–7
John 6:16–21

Working for Those In Need

In today's reading from the Acts of the Apostles
we have a first account of how the Church in Jerusalem
continued to expand in its work for the people,
and how others besides the Twelve
had to be appointed to do it.
The work is something simple to begin with—
the daily distribution of food—
but we know how it continues to expand
in a variety of ways.

There's a story about a Jesuit from India
who was working with the Angolan refugees in Zambia.
Father Sal is his name, short for Salvadore.
Some years ago on Holy Thursday
he got a letter from the Zambian government
telling him he was expelled from the camp
and had to leave the next afternoon, on Good Friday.
He went to the bishops' conference for help.
But none of the bishops were able to get permission
for him to go back to the refugee camp.

Then after six months a saintly woman
who spent much of her time working for lepers
told Father Sal that she would fast for three days
and pray for him. And so she did.

Then she went to see the minister
of the Zambian government, and she said to him:
"When I die the Lord will ask me
what I have done for the lepers.
When you die he will ask you
what you have done for the refugees."
So the minister asked her what she wanted him to do.
She said, "I want you to permit Father Sal
to go back to the refugee camp."
"Bring him here to see me tomorrow," he said.
And though the minister received him,
he said there was nothing he could do;
only the president could lift the ban.
But that prayerful woman then said to him,
"Sit down and write."
And she dictated to him the letter lifting the ban.
Which just goes to show you, Father Sal said,
what holy and prayerful people can do,
when even bishops fail.
The pope was told about what this lady did
and he sent her a letter of thanks.[14]

What this lady did for the refugees
is a very notable expression
of how the work of the Church continues to expand.
As Jesus once said, What we do
for the least of his brethren, we do for him (Matthew 25:40).
What we have to do can be very difficult,
and very frightening too,
as it must be for those working
with refugees forced to flee for their lives.
But every disciple of Jesus,
like the disciples in the gospel riding the rough sea,

---

[14]*Jesuits*, January 1998, "New Assignment: Angola," 109.

In the Light of the Lord   127

must look to Jesus walking, as it were,
on the troubled waters and hear him say,
"It is I; do not be afraid."

Monday

Acts 6:8–15
John 6:22–29

The Work of God

The word "work" comes up in both readings
and links them very effectively.
Stephen is one of the first deacons
appointed "to wait on tables" (Acts 6:2).
Some commentators think "that it is not
the serving of food that is described here
but rather the keeping of accounts
that recorded the distribution of food
to the needy members of the community.
In any case, after Stephen and the others are chosen,
they are never presented as carrying out the task
for which they were appointed."[15]
Rather, as we heard in the first reading,
"Stephen, full of grace and power,
did great wonders and signs among the people" (6:8).

In the gospel, the crowd whom Jesus had fed
with the multiplication of loaves
follows him across the sea, and Jesus tells them:
"Do not work for food that perishes
but for the food that endures for eternal life."
"What must we do," they ask,
"to perform the works of God?"
"This is the work of God," Jesus says,

---

[15]*The New American Bible*, footnote 6:2, 188.

In the Light of the Lord

"that you believe in the one
whom he has sent" (6:26–29).

That is certainly Stephen's work:
he believed in the One whom God has sent
and worked so that others would believe.
To repeat Jesus' words:
"Do not work for food that perishes
but for the food that endures for eternal life."
In other words, believe in Jesus the bread of life,
recognize him in the breaking of the bread,
the bread that comes from God
and gives life to the world.

May we, like Stephen, believe wholeheartedly
in the One whom God has sent
and work so that others may believe.
God give us courage to endure.

Tuesday

Acts 7:51–8:1
John 6:30–35

God's Bread

"The bread of life."
When these words are said at the offertory,
they refer, of course, to the Body of Christ.
But in today's gospel Jesus uses the term
in a somewhat different way.
"I am the bread of life."
And the satisfying of hunger
and the quenching of thirst
is not accomplished by eating and drinking.
It is accomplished rather
by coming to him and believing in him.
"Whoever comes to me will never be hungry,
and whoever believes in me will never be thirsty" (6:35).

Coming to him and believing in him
are one and the same thing.
It is recognizing that Jesus is indeed "God's bread"
come down from heaven to give life to the world.
And this Jesus, now risen from the dead,
returns to heaven to prepare a place for us.

This is Stephen's vision,
moments before he is stoned to death.
As we heard him say in the first reading,
"Look! . . . I see the heavens opened

In the Light of the Lord   131

and the Son of Man standing
at the right hand of God!" (7:55).

Saul witnessed Stephen's death,
he "approved of his execution" (8:1 REB).
But Stephen's words and Stephen's death
seared themselves in his memory,
and Saul becomes Paul when the heavens open,
and death is seen not as the end of everything
but as the beginning of fulfillment in the risen Christ.

In a way all this resonates with the opening prayer:
"Father, you open the kingdom of heaven
to those born again by water and the Spirit.
Increase your gift of love to us.
May all who have been freed from sins in baptism
receive all that you have promised.
Through our Lord Jesus Christ, your Son."

Wednesday *Acts 8:1–8*
John 6:35–40

Hunger and Thirst

One of the most zealous persecutors
of the Church in Jerusalem was a man named Saul.
As we heard in the first reading,
he entered house after house,
dragged men and women out,
and threw them into jail (8:3).
This Saul, of course, becomes Paul,
one of the most effective of apostles,
even though he says of himself,
"I am the least of the apostles,
unfit to be called an apostle,
because I persecuted the church of God" (1 Corinthians 15:9).
The persecution was so severe
that many of the Christians fled to Samaria,
including the deacon Philip, and this resulted
in the conversion of a good number of Samaritans.

Even in the time of Jesus, many of the Samaritans
who lived in a town near Jacob's well
began to believe in him. Why?
Because the woman who had met Jesus at the well
testified to them that he had told her
everything she had done (John 4:39).
Something else that he had told her
resonates with what we hear him say

in today's gospel. He tells her,
"[T]hose who drink of the water that I will give them
will never be thirsty. The water that I will give
will become in them a spring of water
gushing up to eternal life" (4:14).
In today's gospel Jesus tells the people
who had followed him across the sea,
"I am the bread of life.
Whoever comes to me will never be hungry,
and whoever believes in me will never be thirsty" (6:35).

It may seem a bit puzzling
that Jesus juxtaposes hunger and thirst
even though he mentions only bread, not water.
But calling himself the bread of life
is a foreshadowing of the Eucharist,
which involves both flesh and blood,
and therefore satisfies both hunger and thirst.

Thanks be to God for the many gifts he has given us,
especially the bread of life and the cup of salvation.

Thursday

Faith Seeking Understanding

Saint Anselm, a theologian of the eleventh century,
often spoke of faith seeking understanding,
of the soul standing "on tiptoe to see more."
But God dwells in "inaccessible light"
and we can only see so much.
He uses the analogy of the sun:
We can't look at it directly
but we can see everything by its light.[16]

There is also the Son that comes down from heaven:
the Son of God. In his light we see light.
As we heard in today's gospel: "No one can come to me
unless drawn by the Father who sent me" (6:44).

The Ethiopian, in today's first reading,
is already being drawn. We can sense in him
a clear instance of "faith seeking understanding."
God inspires Philip to go to him and explain Isaiah,
the book that he was reading at the time.
After which, the Ethiopian asks,
"What's to keep me from being baptized?"
Baptism: he thereby enters the church,
receives new life in Jesus.
And what will sustain this life?

---

[16]*The Liturgy of the Hours II*, 1774-75.

In the Light of the Lord

Jesus himself will. "I am the living bread
that came down from heaven"—
yes, the Word made flesh—
"and the bread that I will give
is my flesh for the life of the world" (6:51).

With this verse John has Jesus pronounce
a clear statement of the Eucharist.
In John's account of the Last Supper,
Jesus doesn't pronounce the words of institution.
But these words are much the same.
The Eucharist: to sustain life, to satisfy
our hunger and thirst for God.
As we say in the refrain of that eucharistic song:
"You satisfy the hungry heart with gift of finest wheat.
Come give us, O saving Lord, the bread of life to eat."[17]

---

[17]Robert E. Kreutz, "Gift of Finest Wheat."

Friday

Holy Communion

Of the four evangelists, John is the only one
who does not speak of the Eucharist at the Last Supper.
He has Jesus washing the feet of his disciples
and giving his farewell discourse,
but says nothing about the Eucharist as such.
Today's gospel, plausibly enough, is the reason why.
He has Jesus describe the Eucharist in great detail.

"In this description of the eucharist
as 'eating flesh and drinking blood,'
'flesh and blood' is a Hebrew idiom
for the whole person
so that the sense is: sacramental communion
is a personal communion (encounter) with Jesus
who shares his life
and the life of his Father with us (6:53) . . .
[I]n the eucharist Jesus continues
that life-giving mission
which he had received from his Father
and he communicates the life
he receives from his Father,
who is the source of all 'life'" (6:57).[18]

"Just as the living Father sent me,
and I live because of the Father,

[18]McPolin, *John*, 107.

In the Light of the Lord   137

so whoever eats me
will live because of me" (6:57).

This life-giving mission is given to the apostles.
And as we heard in the first reading,
Paul, very dramatically, is called to be an apostle,
an apostle for the Gentiles
but also for the people of Israel.
After he recovered his sight,
he got up and was baptized.
He stayed some time with the disciples
and then began to proclaim in the synagogues
that Jesus was the Son of God,
that is, that Jesus had life from the Father
and was sent to share it with us all.

The opening prayer is a good way of expressing this,
and so we would do well to say it again:
"Father, by the love of your Spirit,
may we who have experienced
the grace of the Lord's resurrection
rise to the newness of life in joy."

Saturday

Acts 9:31–42
John 6:60–69

Faith and Love

Faith is not something we can take for granted.
Faith is not something fixed and finished
after our first declaration of it.
Faith is something ongoing,
something regularly refueled, like love,
a relationship between the one believing
and the one in whom we believe.

In the first reading, we hear that many
came to believe in the Lord; in the gospel,
there were some who did not believe.

In the first reading from the Acts of the Apostles,
one of Peter's acts is truly amazing.
He kneels down and prays over a disciple who had died,
and then he says to her, "Tabitha, get up" (9:40).
That name brings to mind what Jesus said
to the little girl he raised from the dead,
"*Talitha, cum,*" which means,
"Little girl, get up!" (Mark 5:41)
Tabitha opens her eyes, sees Peter, and sits up.
That's when many come to believe in the Lord.
A miracle like that certainly inspires faith.
What will it take to sustain it?

In the gospel, Jesus, we're told, knew
that his disciples were murmuring
about something he had said.
"Does this offend you?" he asks (6:61).
In yesterday's gospel, and the day before yesterday,
he had said that he was the living bread
that had come down from heaven;
and that whoever eats this bread will live forever.
Some of his disciples found this a hard saying.
Some of you, Jesus said, ". . . do not believe."
As a result of this, many of them, we're told,
"turned back and no longer went about with him" (6:64, 66).
That's when Jesus puts this question to the Twelve:
"Do you also wish to go away?"
To which Peter answers:
"Lord, to whom can we go?
You have the words of eternal life.
We have come to believe
and know that you are the Holy One of God" (6:67–69).

May the Lord sustain our faith.
May he refuel it with his love.

Monday

Acts 11:1–18
John 10:1–10

The Gate of God

To appreciate what Jesus is saying in the gospel,
it's helpful to again remind ourselves
that Jesus has two kinds of sheepfolds in mind.
There were commercial sheepfolds in the villages,
with strong gates and watchful gatekeepers,
and if a shepherd with his sheep was close enough
to a village when night fell, he would take them there.
This is the kind of sheepfold that Jesus refers to first.
He's not the gate but the shepherd of the sheep
for whom the gate is opened.

The second kind of sheepfold
is just an open space in the wilderness
enclosed by a circle of piled-up rocks.
And the shepherd lays himself down across the opening
to stop any thief or wild animal from entering.[19]
This is what Jesus has in mind when he says,
"I am the gate.
Whoever enters by me will be saved,
and will come in and go out and find pasture.
The thief comes only to steal and kill and destroy;
I came that they may have life,
and have it abundantly" (John 10:9–10).

---

[19]Joseph A. Tetlow, S.J., "Accurate Image," *America*, May 2, 1980, 373.

Life in abundance is life in the Spirit.
When Peter in the first reading justifies
his entering the house of Gentiles
and eating with them, he says it was because
the Holy Spirit came upon them,
"just as it had upon us at the beginning,"
apparently referring to the experience of Pentecost.
If God, he says, "gave them the same gift he gave us
when we believed in the Lord Jesus Christ,"
meaning of course their faith in the risen Christ,
then who was I to stand in God's way? (11:15, 17)

When Peter's accusers hear this,
they stop objecting, we're told,
and instead began to praise God,
which is another way of saying "Alleluia."

And we keep saying it too, Alleluia,
because God gives to us now
what he gave to the Gentiles then,
life in the Spirit,
through Jesus Christ, the one true Gate of God.

In the Light of the Lord

Monday (Yr A)

Acts 11:1–18
John 10:11–18

Knowing and Loving

When an actor's friend had died, the actor
was asked to read Psalm 23 at his friend's wake.
"The LORD is my shepherd,
I shall not want."
He read it from beginning to end
and it was very impressive.
Then the grandmother was asked
if she wanted to say anything.
Now, the grandmother was deaf,
so she hadn't heard what the actor had read.
And she immediately recited by heart the same psalm.
Her recitation was even more impressive
than the actor's, and when he was asked
why he thought she was so impressive,
he said, "I know the psalm; she knows the shepherd."

"I am the good shepherd," Jesus says,
"and I know my own and my own know me,
just as the Father knows me
and I know the Father . . ." (10:14–15).
What way is that? we might ask.[20]
How does the Father know the Son
and the Son the Father?
The answer must be,
He knows the Son because he loves him.

[20]*The Paths of Life, Cycle B*, 83.

In the Light of the Lord   143

We are more likely to say:
The more you know a person the more you love him.
But it is truer to say:
The more you love a person the more you know him.

Saint Gregory the Great simply takes this for granted.
He has Jesus say: "I am the Good Shepherd.
I know my own—by which I mean, I love them—
and my own know me." Later on Gregory adds:
"I assure you that it is not by faith
that you will come to know him, but by love."[21]

Jesus shows his love for us
by laying down his life for us.
For the sheep, we hear him say,
"I lay down my life."
Then he follows that with: "I have other sheep
that do not belong to this fold.
I must bring them also,
and they will listen to my voice . . ." (10:15–16)

This confirms what we hear in the first reading,
how Peter is instructed to go like a shepherd
to the Gentiles and to bring them,
like other sheep, into the fold.
"If then God gave them the same gift he gave us"—
namely, the Holy Spirit—
"when we believed in the Lord Jesus Christ,
who was I," says Peter, "that I could hinder God?" (11:17)

May we love Jesus more ardently
so that we may know him more intimately.

---

[21]*The Liturgy of the Hours II*, 752-753.

In the Light of the Lord

Tuesday

Eternal Life

To know:
this is one of the greatest of gifts.
To know another person:
this is one of the greatest of privileges.
To be known:
this is one of the deepest desires of the heart.
To be known as we are and yet to be loved.
To be loved because of what we are.
With a love that by its very nature
makes us better than we are
because it awakens in us
all that is good and loving and true.

In today's gospel Jesus uses the image
of the shepherd and his sheep.
He says he knows his sheep
and because they know him they follow him.
"I give them eternal life,
and they will never perish.
No one will snatch them out of my hand" (10:28).
One of the great scenes depicted in mosaics
of the early Church is Christ's descent into hell,
his descent, that is, into the realm of death,
there to claim those who are his.

"My Father who has given them to me
is greater than all,
and no one can snatch them out of the Father's care.
The Father and I are one" (10:29–30 REB).

To know God, "the only true God,"
and Jesus Christ whom God has sent:
that, John has Jesus say at the Last Supper,
"is eternal life" (John 17:3).
And Jesus wants us to live that life.
That's the wonder of it all.
That's the gist of the last words of his priestly prayer:
"I made your name known to them
and I will make it known,
so that the love with which you loved me
may be in them, and I in them" (17:26).

Thanks be to God,
for the greatest of gifts,
for the greatest of privileges,
for fulfillment of the deepest desire of our hearts.[22]

---

[22]Adapted from the author's *The Paths of Life, Cycle C*, 80-81.

In the Light of the Lord

Wednesday

Acts 12:24–13:5
John 12:44–50

Light From Light

"The Book of Signs" and "The Book of Glory":
those are the two major parts of John's gospel.
What John has Jesus say in today's reading
is the last public teaching of the Book of Signs.
It's "a summary of his mission,"
of what he was sent to do,
"and a summons to faith,"[23]
to faith with greater understanding.
But this faith reaches through Jesus to the Father.
"I have come as light into the world," he says (12:46).
He comes as Light from Light.
As we're told in Psalm 36,
"[I]n your light we see light" (36:9).
In Jesus we see the Father.
In Jesus we hear the Father.
"I have not spoken on my own";
no, "the Father who sent me
has himself given me a commandment
about what to say and what to speak.
And I know that his commandment
is eternal life" (12:49).

"Commandment" here is not what we ordinarily think,
like "Do this, or you'll be punished."

---

[23]McPolin, *John*, 177.

No, it's more like the command to breathe.
"Breathe, if you want to live."
"Believe, if you want to live"—
to live the life of God.

With this in mind,
let us say again the opening prayer,
one of the most beautiful of Easter prayers.
"God our Father,
life of the faithful,
glory of the humble,
happiness of the just,
hear our prayer.
Fill our emptiness
with the blessing of this eucharist,
the foretaste of eternal joy."

Thursday

One and the Same

For the next three weeks we'll we hearing again
some of those powerful and mysterious words,
in the gospel according to John,
that Jesus speaks in his discourse at the Last Supper.
The Eucharist is, after all,
a reenactment of the Last Supper,
and even though these words are given to us
before his passion and death,
they resonate now with his resurrection.

One of the things that John says of Jesus
before Jesus begins speaking is:
He knew "that he had come from God
and was going to God" (13:3).
Today's first reading corresponds
to the first part of this statement,
and the conclusion of the gospel
corresponds to the second part.

The correspondence has to do with a path of life
that is traced in each reading.
In the first reading Paul is speaking in the synagogue
to his fellow Israelites
and "others who fear God" (13:16).
And he traces a path of life in the history of his people

from God to Abraham to Moses
to Samuel to Saul to David,
and then to John the Baptist
who heralds the coming of Jesus.
From God to Jesus.
As is said of Jesus,
He knew that he had come from God.

In the gospel Jesus concludes with these words:
"Very truly, I tell you,
whoever receives one whom I send receives me;
and whoever receives me
receives him who sent me" (13:20).
This is to trace a path of life from the apostles,
from missionaries, from ministers,
from anyone whom Jesus sends,
to Jesus, and from Jesus to God, the one who sent him.

The path of life in the first reading
and the path of life in the gospel
are one and the same, of course.
It's just that we see it from different points of view.
In the first reading Jesus comes to us from God;
in the second Jesus goes back to God,
and we go with him.

In the Light of the Lord

Friday

Acts 13:26–33
John 14:1–6

Embrace and Release

There is a time for embracing
and a time for releasing.
But before one time ends
and the other begins,
there is a moment when embrace and release
converge in the same act
and are never more keenly felt.

That act is the act of parting,
the parting of one person from another,
or more than one from one or more.
"Parting," says Emily Dickinson—
she says this in one of her poems—
"Parting is all we know of heaven,
and all we need of hell."[24]
At that moment of parting,
love overflows the heart,
but how painful the sense of loss!

Jesus and his disciples
experience such a moment at the Last Supper.
Lord, says Thomas, "we do not know
where you are going.
How can we know the way?" (14:5)

---

[24]"My Life Closed Twice."

But even as Jesus refers to his time for release,
he promises embrace.
"I am the way, and the truth, and the life.
No one comes to the Father except through me" (14:6).
Jesus knows that he comes from God
and that he is going back to God.
He is ready to release his very self into God's embrace.

As we hear Paul say in the first reading,
what God promised our ancestors
he has brought to fulfillment for us, their children.
How? By raising up Jesus,
an event foretold in the words of the psalm:
"You are my Son;
today I have begotten you" (13:32–33).
The Father's love will create him anew.
With this hope in his heart,
Jesus says to his disciples:
"Do not let your hearts be troubled.
Believe in God; believe also in me" (John 14:1).[25]

---

[25]Adapted from the author's *Gospel Journey*, 87-88.

Saturday

Acts 13:44–52
John 14:7–14

To the Ends of the Earth

In the gospel we hear Philip, one of the Twelve,
ask Jesus to do something that, according to Jesus,
had already been done: "[S]how us the Father,"
he says, "[and that will indeed be enough for us]" (14:8).
Philip comes up more than once in John's gospel.
Jesus meets him in Galilee and says to him,
"Follow me" (1:43);
and Philip shows such a readiness to believe in him
that he goes to Nathanael and says,
"We have found the man
of whom Moses wrote in the law,
the man foretold by the prophets;
it is Jesus son of Joseph, from Nazareth" (1:45 REB).
And apparently his close association with Jesus
was very evident, because on one occasion
some Greeks came up to him and said to him,
"Sir, we wish to see Jesus" (12:21).

The same Philip who says to Jesus,
"Show us the Father,
[and that will indeed be enough for us,]"
uses the word "enough" on a previous occasion.
In the preparation for feeding the five thousand,
it was Philip who said to Jesus,
Not even "[s]ix months' wages" would be "enough"
to get a little bit of food for each of them (John 6:7).

In the Light of the Lord   153

As one commentator puts it, "Jesus' mighty deed
on that occasion should have taught Philip
to revise his estimate of what 'is enough.'
He has yet to realize that to 'know' Jesus
is in reality a never ending process."[26]
"Have I have been with you all this time, Philip."
said Jesus, "and you still do not know me?
Whoever has seen me has seen the Father.
How can you say, 'Show us the Father'?" (14:9)

Jesus then says something rather astounding
which resonates with what Paul and Barnabas
are said to have done in the first reading.
"Very truly, I tell you, the one who believes in me
will also do the works that I do,
and, in fact, will do greater works than these,
because I am going to the Father" (14:12).
One of the works of Jesus is certainly his teaching,
and it becomes a greater work when it reaches out
not only to the Jews but to the Gentiles as well.
As we heard Paul say in the first reading,
"For so the Lord has commanded us, saying,
'I have set you to be a light for the Gentiles,
so that you may bring salvation
to the ends of the earth'" (13:47).
And he and Barnabas, expelled by the Jews,
go to the Gentiles in Iconium
and establish a church there
separate from the synagogue. And they
"were filled with joy and with the Holy Spirit" (13:52).

In response to what we hear,
we would do well to say again:

---

[26]David M. Stanley, S.J., "*I Encountered God!*," 223.

"All the ends of the earth have seen
the salvation of our God.
Sing joyfully to the LORD, all you lands;
break into song; sing praise" (Psalm 98:3–4).

Monday

Acts 14:5–18
John 14:21–26

Jesus Revealed

Paul and Barnabas have been traveling
on their first missionary journey
from town to town in Asia Minor.
We meet them in today's first reading in Lystra,
where they had fled when both Jews and Gentiles
in another town had attempted to stone them.
In Lystra there was a man crippled from birth
who listened to Paul preaching.
Paul looked at him, saw faith in him, and cured him.
When the people saw what he had done, they cried out:
"The gods have come down to us in human form!"
Barnabas they called "Zeus,"
the greatest of Greek gods,
and Paul they called "Hermes," a spokesman for Zeus,
since Paul was clearly the chief speaker (14:11–12).

No doubt they had in mind that legend
told by the Roman poet Ovid.
Zeus and Hermes had come in disguise to Lystra.
The people treated them with contempt,
and for that reason the two gods punished them.
And so it's as if the people of Lystra
weren't taking any chances this time.[27]
Paul and Barnabas responded in protest:
We're not gods, they said; we're humans like you!

[27]See Mark Link, *Mission 2000, B Cycle*, 144.

And they told them about the one living God.
But not a word about Jesus.
Yet when Paul was preaching,
and he saw faith in that cripple,
he must have been talking about Jesus.

In a sense, this seems to raise the question
which one of the apostles named Judas
(not Judas Iscariot) brings up in today's gospel:
Lord, why is it that you "reveal yourself
to us, and not to the world?"
And Jesus answers: "Those who love me
will keep my word, and my Father will love them,
and we will come to them
and make our home with them" (14:22–23).

Jesus' answer is not immediately clear.
He seems to be saying that "the answer
to Judas's question is in Judas's hands."[28]
If Judas and the other disciples—
and Paul and Barnabas, and you and me—
keep Jesus' word,
Jesus will show himself to the world.
Keep his word. What word?
In the light of what he said,
the word is the command to love.
If they, if we, love one another
as Jesus loves them and us,
then Jesus will indeed be revealed to the world,
and the Father in him.
This is, after all, the world that the Father so loved
that he sent his only Son.

---

[28]Michael Fallon, *The Winston Commentary on the Gospels*, 388.

Loving one another, in deed and truth,
and not just talking about it,
is apparently the best form of preaching.

Tuesday

Acts 14:19–28
John 14:27–31

Peace

There had probably been less peace
in the twentieth century than in any other.
"Too often," Pope John Paul II once said,
"violence seems to be the easiest formula
for resolving difficult situations."
And he condemned "every form of violence,
ethnic cleansing, deportation of people,
and the exclusion of peoples from social life."[29]

" 'Peace' is my farewell to you,"
we hear Jesus say to his disciples in the gospel.
Peace, *shalom*—that's a traditional Hebrew greeting.
But like *goodbye* it can become minimal in meaning.
Goodbye means "God be with you,"
but we rarely say it with that in mind.

---

[29]*The Tablet*, May 1, 1999.

"My peace," Jesus says, "I give to you.
I do not give to you as the world gives to you" (14:27).
Not just as the end or the absence of war,
desirable as that may be.
No, Jesus gives it as communion with God:
Jesus is himself our peace and reconciliation;
in Jesus we live in peace with God and one another.

Why are we so often not at peace?
In the first reading, Paul is stoned by the very people
who had called him a god
when he cured a man lame from birth.
They stoned him
when they were won over by the Jews from Antioch.
Christ our peace can paradoxically
be the cause of strife and division,
if his good news is rejected:
"I have come to bring not peace but the sword"
(Matthew 10:34).

Gerard Manley Hopkins has a poem called "Peace."
Peace, he says, is like a wild wooddove
that keeps roaming round him,
but when will it alight on his boughs?
"When, when, Peace, will you, Peace?. . .
I yield you do come sometimes, but
That piecemeal peace is poor peace."
In place of peace, he says, the Lord leaves patience,
which "plumes to peace hereafter."

Jesus speaks very frankly
about the trials and tribulations
that believers will experience
in their journey through the world.

"I have said this to you,
so that in me you may have peace.
In the world you face persecution.
But take courage;
I have conquered the world!" (John 16:33).

Paul assures us that "the peace of God,
which surpasses all understanding,
will guard your hearts and your minds
in Christ Jesus" (Philippians 4:7).
Shalom! Come, Peace!
Come, Lord Jesus!

Wednesday

Acts 15:1–6
John 15:1–8

The Vine and The Branches

During the war years when I was still in my teens,
my father planted a grape vine.
And I remember how one year he had a man come over
and graft new branches onto the vine,
which produced a lot of grapes
from which my father made good wine.

What brings this to mind
is Saint Paul in today's first reading
preaching to the Gentiles and converting them.
Later, in his letter to the Romans (11:17–24),
he would describe how the Gentiles were grafted
in the place of the natural branches
which had been broken off because of their unbelief.
These natural branches were, of course, the Jews
who will, says Saint Paul, one day be grafted back!

What is important is this vital connection with Christ:
He is the vine, we are the branches.
Some of the Jews who became Christians
were insisting that the Gentiles be circumcised
and keep the Mosaic Law.
But no, Paul would say, and Peter and all the apostles,
what is essential is faith in the risen Christ,
which grafts us into the very source of life
and makes us fruitful.

"Abide in me, as I abide in you.
Just as the branch cannot bear fruit by itself
unless it abides in the vine,
neither can you unless you abide in me" (John 15:4).
And the opposite is also true:
The vine can't bear fruit without its branches.
Just as the vine needs its branches, so Christ needs us.
The one thing necessary is that we stay connected.
May all of us, natural branches and grafted branches,
live in him who is the true vine.

In the Light of the Lord

Thursday

Acts 15:7–21
John 15:9–11

The Cause of Our Joy

Today's gospel comes from what is called
Jesus' last discourse.
He spoke it at the Last Supper,
but here we are reading it after his resurrection.
Readings from the last discourse
began in the middle of the Fourth Week,
and they'll continue up to Pentecost.
What is the reason for this?
According to Raymond Brown, even though historically
this discourse is set at the Last Supper,
it really goes beyond the Last Supper:
it's envisioning the Church of the future,
the Church of all time, and therefore
it has this direct, almost personal, address.
Now and then a disciple may ask a question,
but for the most part Jesus is addressing a "you."
And the "you" becomes not only those
at the supper table but those beyond.

To help us understand,
Raymond Brown suggests that we imagine
Leonardo da Vinci's vision of the supper table
where a lot of the disciples are drawn up
and interacting with one another.
You can stage this, he says,

by having Jesus there in the midst of his disciples
with the audience all around them.
And although the audience is somewhat in the dark
because they're looking at the stage,
Jesus is talking as much to the audience
as he is talking to those who are there at the table.
"It's that kind of effect. And [Jesus] is praying.
He prays specifically: 'I pray for you,
and I pray for those who believe in me on your word.'
And it's clear he's reaching out to them as well."[30]

To them, to those who believe in him,
and therefore to us.
As we hear Jesus say in today's gospel,
"As the Father has loved me,
so I have loved you;
abide in my love."
And how do we abide in his love?
"If you keep my commandments,
you will abide in my love,
just as I have kept my Father's commandments
and abide in his love" (15:9–10).
His commandments. What are his commandments?
I think we have to recognize that his commandments
are all summed up into one.
As he said earlier at the Last Supper:
"I give you a new commandment,
that you love one another. Just as I have loved you,
you also should love one another" (John 13:34).

And this is certainly the cause of our joy.
"I have said these things to you
so that my joy may be in you,
and that your joy may be complete" (15:11).

[30]*The Gospel of John*, tape 9.

In the Light of the Lord

Friday

Acts 15:22–31
John 15:12–17

The Gift of God's Love

The opening words of today's gospel
repeat what Jesus declared earlier in the Last Supper
to be his "new commandment:
that you love one another. As I have loved you,
you also should love one another" (John 13:34).
This is a tremendous gift: Christ's love for us.
And there's an inner dynamic in this gift:
It must be shared.

The first reading is a good account of this sharing.
It follows immediately upon yesterday's reading
from Acts, in which Peter declares himself
to be the one from whose lips "the Gentiles
would hear the message of the good news
and become believers" (15:7).
This is a remarkable declaration.
It goes against the belief of centuries:
that the gift of God's love resided in Israel alone.
God chose Israel not for herself alone
but precisely for her to cherish,
and to share with all peoples,
the revelation of his love,
especially as that love is revealed
in the person of Jesus Christ.
This is something we must all take to heart.

The gospel reiterates and elaborates
the same unchanging message:
God in his love gives and shares.
God's gift, therefore, must be shared.
Jesus tells his disciples:
"As the Father has loved me, so I have loved you" (15:9).
It follows then that we must "love one another"
as he has loved us.
There is more: "You did not choose me," he says,
"but I chose you."
Why? Is this gift of his favor meant for us alone?
No. He chose us, he says, "to go and bear fruit."
And so he says yet again:
"I am giving you these commands
so that you may love one another" (15:12–17).

Saturday

Acts 16:1–10
John 15:18–21

The Light of the World

The "world." This is a word John uses very frequently
in his gospel. He doesn't always use it the same way,
but often enough it simply means the "world of people."
And this is the world we hear a lot about
in today's first reading from the Acts of the Apostles.
Paul on his second missionary journey
travels from north to west in Asia Minor.
He meets the disciple Timothy in Lystra
and goes with him from town to town,
proclaiming the good news to the people.
At a town by the sea Paul has a vision,
a vision of a man imploring him to cross over
to Macedonia; and when he decides to go,
he crosses over to another part of the world,
to the world of people called Europe.

Yes, that's a frequent meaning of the word "world"
in John's gospel, like when the Samaritans say
that Jesus is "the Savior of the world" (4:42),
when Jesus says he is "the light of the world" (8:12),
when John declares that "God so loved the world
that he gave his only Son . . ." (3:16).
But many times in the latter part of his gospel,
as in today's reading, the word "world" is used
to categorize "those who reject faith in Jesus,

who oppose and persecute him and his followers."[31]
"If the world hates you," Jesus says,
be aware that it hated me before" (15:18).
There was a lot of hatred and persecution going on
when John wrote this gospel,
and it's still going on in countries around the world.
In this context we would do well to remember
the last of the beatitudes that Jesus taught
in his Sermon on the Mount:
"Blessed are you when people revile you
and persecute you and utter all kinds of evil
against you [falsely] on my account.
Rejoice and be glad,
for your reward will be great in heaven" (Matthew 5:11).

Jesus, the light of the world:
We also, you said, are "the light of the world."
May our light "shine before others,
so that they may see [our] good works
and give glory to [our] Father in heaven" (Matthew 5:14, 16).

---

[31]George W. MacRae, *Invitation to John*, 187.

Monday

Acts 16:11–15
John 15:26–16:4

Witness

The first words of Jesus to his disciples,
"When the Paraclete comes," or "Advocate,"
as the *New Revised Standard Version* Bible has it,
bring to mind the great feast of Pentecost,
when we celebrate the coming of the Holy Spirit.
Paraclete means "called to the side
of one in need of assistance. . ."[32]
The general meaning of the word is helper.
The Holy Spirit is a helper
because, as "the Spirit of Truth," Jesus says,
he will bear witness (or testify) on my behalf.
And in the very next sentence, Jesus tells the disciples
that *they* will bear witness (or testify) on his behalf.
And so, although the witnessing
is to be that of the disciples, "it is the Spirit
who will empower them to carry it out."[33]

In the first reading from Acts
we certainly see the disciples in action.
Paul had had a vision: A Macedonian
had stood before him and said: "Come and help us."
And so he and Luke cross the sea to Macedonia,
and following the Roman road,
they reach the city of Philippi.

[32]*Dictionary of the Bible*, 636.
[33]George W. MacRae, *Invitation to John*, 188.

In the Light of the Lord　　　169

There they meet a number of women
on the bank of the river;
and one of them, a prominent woman named Lydia,
listens with an open heart to what Paul is saying
and how he is helping them
by bearing witness to Christ.
After she and her household are baptized,
she offers Paul and Luke an invitation.
"If you have judged me to be faithful to the Lord,"
"come and stay at my home." And that they do.

Paul's witnessing in Philippi
is very happy and peaceful.
A time will come when witnessing to Christ,
for Paul and others, is not so peaceful.
As we hear Jesus say in the gospel,
A time will come when "those who kill you
will think that by doing so
they are offering worship to God" (16:2).
John the evangelist is writing this
toward the end of the first century,
but it's not until the second century
that the Greek word for witness, *martys,*
is used to designate one who suffers death
for witnessing to Christ—a martyr, as we say.

May the Spirit of Truth help us to witness to Christ
and move all those to whom we witness
to listen, like Lydia, with an open heart.

Tuesday
Acts 16:22–34
John 16:5–11

The Presence of Christ Through the Spirit

As we draw closer to the Ascension and to Pentecost,
we, of course, begin to hear much more
about the Paraclete, the Advocate, the Holy Spirit.
The risen Christ
is no longer physically present in a place;
he is present to us through the Spirit
wherever we may be.
The presence of Christ through the Spirit
is implied in the first reading
and declared in the second.
And, not surprisingly, it's made mention of
in autobiographical or confessional readings of saints.

As in the Confessions of Saint Patrick,
to start with one of the saints.
At sixteen Patrick was captured by pirates.
He was brought to Ireland and sold as a slave.
For six years he was forced to shepherd
his master's flocks.
And during all that time he taught himself to pray.
". . . I used to stay in the woods," he writes,
"and on the mountains,
and I used to get up for prayer before daylight,

In the Light of the Lord   171

through snow, through frost, through rain,
and I felt no harm, nor sloth . . .
because the Spirit was fervent within [me]."[34]

We can surely say much the same thing
of Paul and Silas in today's first reading:
The Spirit was fervent within them.
There they are in prison,
having been stripped and flogged,
and they're praying and singing hymns to God.

The Spirit was fervent within them. Christ's spirit.
"[I]f I do not go away," Jesus says to his disciples
in the gospel, "the [Spirit] will not come to you" (16:7).

According to theologian David Stanley,
the "astounding truth" is that the risen Lord,
by his Spirit, "is more dynamically present . . .
to the community of faith
than ever he was 'in the days of his flesh.'"[35]

To quote Saint Patrick again,
"Christ with me, Christ before me, Christ behind me,
Christ in me, Christ beneath me, Christ above me,
Christ on my right, Christ on my left,
Christ where I lie, Christ where I sit,
Christ where I arise."

The all-encompassing presence of Christ
through the Spirit.

---

[34]Quoted, in part, in *Mission 2000, B Cycle,* 152.
[35]*"I Encountered God!,"* 274.

In the Light of the Lord

Wednesday

Acts 17:15, 22–18:1
John 16:12–15

The Spirit of Truth

Jesus knew he had come from God
and was going back to God.
"[I]f I do not go away, the [Spirit] will not come to you,"
as he said in yesterday's gospel (16:7).
And in today's gospel
Jesus calls him "the Spirit of truth" (16:13),
a Spirit who will guide us to all truth,
a Spirit who will not speak on his own,
just as Jesus did not.

The Spirit searches everything,
even the depths of God (1 Corinthians 2).
With regard to human beings,
who knows what's within a person?
Only the spirit of that person knows.
So it is with the Spirit of God.
The Spirit, Jesus says, "will declare to you
the things that are to come" (16:13).
According to more than one commentator,
this is not a reference to new predictions
about the future, but an interpretation
of what has already been said.[36]
Jesus has already predicted his death and resurrection.

---

[36]See *The New American Bible*, footnote 16:13, 170, and Raymond E. Brown, *The Gospel According to John*, vol. 29A, 701, 715-716.

In the Light of the Lord   173

It is the Spirit that will teach us
the significance of it all—
what it meant for Christ, what it means for us:
Christ risen, Christ exalted.

This is the climax of Paul's preaching
to the people of Athens,
as we heard in the first reading.
God has raised Jesus from the dead
(though Paul doesn't use the name of Jesus yet).
The response of his Greek listeners was mixed:
some scoffed; others said,
"We will hear you again about this,"
but a few followed him and believed (17:32–34).

Only the Spirit can guide us into all the truth.
As Jesus says, the Spirit "will take
what is mine and declare it to you.
All that the Father has is mine" (16:14–15).

In response to what Jesus says,
I find it appropriate to conclude
with this last verse of a hymn:
"For the wonders that astound us,
For the truths that still confound us,
Most of all, that love has found us,
Thanks be to God."[37]

---

[37]F. Pratt Green, *The Liturgy of the Hours II*, 1171.

In the Light of the Lord

Ascension Thursday
Acts 1:1–11; Ephesians 1:17–23
(Yr A): Matthew 28:16–20
(Yr B): Mark 16:15–20
(Yr C): Luke 24:46–53

The Love That Moves the Sun

Consider that splendid line
that ends Dante's *Divine Comedy*:
"the Love that moves the sun and the other stars."
That love is the motive force in the great drama
of creation and redemption.
The Ascension is the next to last moment in the drama,
the last being the sending of the Holy Spirit,
an end which is itself a beginning.
Liturgically, we move from Advent to Pentecost,
from the promise of Jesus, the first "Advocate,"
to the promise of "another": "I will ask the Father,"
Jesus says at the Last Supper, "and he will give you
another Advocate, to be with you forever" (John 14:16).

The Ascension keeps that promise before us.
In the first reading, Jesus enjoins his disciples
to wait for " 'the promise of the Father.
This' he says, 'is what you have heard from me.' " (Acts 1:4).
And in Luke's gospel he says: "I am sending
upon you what my Father promised" (24:49).
What will the Father do for us
in fulfilling his promise to send the Spirit?
The second reading from Ephesians

supplies us with an answer:
"[T]he God of our Lord Jesus Christ,
the Father of glory,"
will "give you a spirit of wisdom and revelation
as you come to know him," will enlighten
the eyes of your heart "that you may know
what is the hope to which he has called you,
what are the riches of his glorious inheritance . . .
and what is the immeasurable greatness of his power
for us who believe . . ." (1:17–19).

This power, like God's strength
in raising Jesus from the dead
and placing him over all creation,
this power has "put all things under his feet"
and has made him head of the church,
"which is his body, the fullness of him
who fills all in all" (1:20–23).

Here then is the last ongoing act of the drama
in which we, by virtue of our faith, take part.
The love that moves the sun and the other stars
moves in us and, through us, to all creation:
"Go into all the world," Jesus says in Mark's gospel,
"and proclaim the goods news to the whole creation" (16:15).
In his encyclical *Redemptoris Missio*
(*The Redeemer's Mission*), Pope John Paul
declares that missionary activity
is "a fundamental commitment
of the whole people of God."
At the same time, "the witness of a Christian life
is the first and irreplaceable form of mission" (no. 42).

Thank God we are not left to our own resources.

In the Light of the Lord

"[B]ehold," says the Lord in Matthew's gospel
just before he ascends to the Father,
"I am with you always,
to the end of the age" (28:20).[38]

Friday

Acts 18:9–18
John 16:20–23

Open Wide the Doors to Christ

Nine days—"a novena of expectation"
between Ascension Thursday and Pentecost[39]
(even though in many dioceses
the celebration of the Ascension
is transferred to the following Sunday.)
Whatever the number of days,
it's a time for prayer and reflection.
And as we recall the readings of the day,
some words or phrases will stand out for us.

In the first reading
I stay with what the Lord says to Paul,
"Do not be afraid, . . . for I am with you" (18:9–10).
We've heard this saying before, haven't we?
In fact, I checked to see in the concordance
how many times it occurs in the Scriptures.

[38]Adapted from the author's *The Paths of Life, Cycle A*, 90-92.
[39]*The Vatican II Weekday Missal*, 803.

In the Light of the Lord   177

It occurs dozens of times.
The Lord said the very same words to Isaac:
"[D]o not be afraid, for I am with you." (Genesis 26:24)
Earlier he had said to Isaac's father:
"Do not be afraid, Abram, I am your shield" (15:1).
In Isaiah, the Lord says to Israel:
"[D]o not fear, for I am with you" (41:10).
And Jesus, walking on the water,
says to his disciples: "Take heart,
it is I; do not be afraid" (Matthew 14:27; Mark 6:50; John 6:20).
This is very much like the risen Christ speaking,
speaking to them and to us:
Take heart, do not be afraid.

This relates to what he says in the gospel:
". . . your hearts will rejoice," he says,
"and no one will take your joy from you."
Why? How can this be?
Because, Jesus says, "I will see you again" (John 16:22).

It is the risen Jesus
who comes to see us in the Eucharist.
"Open Wide the Doors to Christ!"
This was a Jubilee exhortation,
but obviously it still holds.
"Open Wide the Doors to Christ!"

In the Light of the Lord

Saturday

Acts 18:23–28
John 16:23–28

Requests Made in the Name of Jesus

Jesus tells us in today's gospel
that whatever we ask the Father in his name,
the Father will give us (16:23).
Earlier he had said he would send us
the Spirit of truth from the Father (15:26),
the Spirit who would guide us to all truth (16:13).
This brings to mind what Saint Paul says
in his letter to the Romans:
"[W]e do not know how to pray as we ought,
but that very Spirit intercedes
with sighs too deep for words" (8:26).

With the coming of the Spirit, we enter
into closer communion with Jesus and the Father,
a closer communion of faith and love.
As a result, requests made in the name of Jesus,
that is, requests which spring
from our communion with him, will be heard.[40]

What requests should we make?
According to theologian Karl Rahner,
we should ask the Father for everything,
"everything that will in any way ease,
clarify, or illuminate our lives";

---

[40]See James McPolin, S.J., *John*, 219.

In the Light of the Lord

we should ask "for our daily bread
and appeal to the eternal Father
in our daily necessities and pain."
Yes, "these things we should do.
But [they] should all be caught up
into the one great prayer of Christ's Spirit,
in the name of Jesus."
The one great prayer is to ask for God;
"on our behalf [the Spirit] asks for God.
Everything is included and contained in this prayer."[41]

As Jesus says, "Ask and you will receive,
so that your joy may be complete" (16:24).

---

[41]*Biblical Homilies*, 85-86.

In the Light of the Lord

Monday

Acts 19:1–8
John 16:29–33

The Gift of the Spirit

We hear the disciples say to Jesus
that there is no need for anyone
to ask him questions (John 16:30).
Do we agree?
I must say today's readings
stir up in me a lot of questions,
so much so that I'm not even sure
how to word them all.
To some disciples in Corinth, Paul puts the question:
"Did you receive the Holy Spirit
when you became believers?" (Acts 19:2)
They say they've never even heard of the Holy Spirit.
How were they baptized?
With the baptism of John.
So then Paul baptizes them
in the name of the Lord Jesus.
"When Paul had laid his hands on them,
the Holy Spirit came upon them . . ." (19:6)
But the laying on of hands is not baptism,
as we know it.
The *Catechism* quotes Pope Paul VI on this question:
"[T]he apostles, in fulfillment of Christ's will,
imparted to the newly baptized
by the laying on of hands
the gift of the Spirit

that completes the grace of Baptism. . . .
The imposition of hands
is rightly recognized by the Catholic tradition
as the origin of the sacrament of Confirmation,
which in a certain way perpetuates
the grace of Pentecost in the Church" (1288).

The disciples in the gospel are believers,
or so they say. They say to Jesus,
We do "believe that you came from God" (16:30).
How would they have answered Paul's question:
"Did you receive the Holy Spirit
when you became believers?" (Acts 19:2)
I guess we can answer for them.
No, they didn't receive the Holy Spirit;
they're still at the Last Supper,
Pentecost for them is yet to come.
So Jesus questions them:
Do you really believe?
The hour is coming when you will scatter
and leave me all alone.
And then Jesus adds:
"I have said this to you,
so that in me you may have peace" (16:33).
What does that mean? How can that be?
To lose faith, or to have it profoundly shaken,
and yet find peace?
Yes, Jesus says, "In the world you face persecution.
But take courage; I have conquered the world!" (16:33).

What Jesus seems to be telling his disciples is,
I know your faith will be shaken,
and because I know it, have faith in me,
and be at peace even as you suffer in the world,

In the Light of the Lord

because I have overcome the world.
How? By the power of the Holy Spirit,
the same Spirit whom I promise to send to you.

Come, faith!
Come, peace!
Come, Holy Spirit!

Tuesday   *Acts 20:17–27*
                                                  John 17:1–11

Now and in the Future

In today's readings both Paul and Jesus
reach an end point in their lives:
Paul has completed an important phase of his ministry,
having worked for two difficult years in Ephesus.
Jesus declares that he has finished the work
that the Father has given him.[42]

Each looks to the future with the confidence
that comes from doing God's will,
with the courage that comes from living God's love.
Paul says to the elders of the Church in Ephesus:
"[A]s a captive to the Spirit, I am on my way to Jerusalem,
not knowing what will happen to me there" (20:22).
Jesus, in his great prayer at the Last Supper, says:
"Father, the hour has come . . .

---

[42]See Stuhlmueller, *Biblical Meditations for the Easter Season*, 127.

In the Light of the Lord   **183**

I have made your name known
to those whom you gave me from the world" (17:1, 6).

Each faces a difficult future.
According to Paul: "[T]he Holy Spirit testifies to me
in every city that imprisonments and persecution
are waiting for me" (20:23).
Jesus, addressing his Father, speaks of his death:
"And now I am no longer in the world,
but they [his disciples] are in the world,
and I am coming to you" (17:11).

Both manifest an interior strength,
a clear conscience, an abiding confidence.

Something that Saint Edith Stein said
before she was martyred at Auschwitz
resonates with the words of Paul and Jesus:
"[I believe] that nothing is merely an accident
when seen in the light of God.
I believe that my whole life . . .
has been marked out for me
in the plan of divine Providence
and has a completely coherent meaning
in God's all-seeing eye."[43]

However difficult our life—
now and in the future—
Christ prays for us.
We pray through him, with him, and in him—
for interior strength, for a clear conscience,
for abiding confidence—and for his Holy Spirit.

---

[43]See Mark Link, *Mission 2000*, 159.

In the Light of the Lord

Wednesday

Acts 20:28–38
John 17:11–19

Consecration in Truth

In today's readings, as in yesterday's,
we hear both Paul and Jesus uttering
some very poignant words of farewell.
Paul, who is leaving Ephesus for good,
tells the elders of the church there
that they must keep watch over the whole flock
which the Holy Spirit has given them to guard.
He addresses them, in effect, as shepherds,
and they must protect the flock
from "savage wolves" (20:28–29).

Jesus, in the gospel, "returns to the attitude
of the Good Shepherd"[44] when he begs the Father
to protect his disciples, "that they may be one,"
just as he and his Father are one (17:11).
Earlier Jesus had said, "I have other sheep
that do not belong to this fold.
I must bring them also. . . .
So there will be one flock, one shepherd" (John 10:16).

Another word comes up in both readings,
the word "consecrate."
Jesus speaks very gently
about consecrating his disciples,

---

[44]Raymond E. Brown, *A Once-and-Coming Spirit at Pentecost*, 93.

In the Light of the Lord   185

and even consecrating himself for them.
And Paul speaks about the inheritance
of all those who have been consecrated.
What exactly does the word "consecrate" mean?
It comes from the Greek word meaning "sacred."
To consecrate someone or another
is to make them sacred,
to make them holy, to sanctify them.

Jesus prays thus for his disciples,
"Consecrate them in the truth;
your word, [Father], is truth.
As you sent me into the world,
I have sent them into the world,
and for their sake I consecrate myself"
(I sanctify myself for them), "so that they too
may be consecrated in truth" (17:17–19 NJB).
When Jesus speaks of sanctifying himself,
he is describing his death.[45]
And Paul says to the elders of the Church:
"And now I commend you to God,
and to the word of his grace that has power
to build you up and to give you your inheritance
among all the sanctified" (20:32 NJB).

May God protect each and every one of us,
so that we may be one as Jesus and the Father are one.
And may God consecrate us in the truth,
so that his gracious word may build us up
and enable us to share in the joy of the Lord.

---

[45]Cf. John 6:51; 10:11, 15; 15:13. *The New Jerome Biblical Commentary*, 979.

In the Light of the Lord

Thursday

Acts 22:30; 23:6–11
John 17:20–26

Life and Love

In the gospel Jesus at the Last Supper
looks up to heaven and prays.
He prays not only for his disciples,
he prays for us too, for all those
who believe in him "through their word."
And what does he pray for?
He prays "that they may all be one,
as you, Father, are in me and I in you."
This prayer of Jesus
has been called his priestly prayer,
precisely because he intercedes for others.
He is truly the Great Reconciler here,
but he is this not only by intercession
but by the sharing of his life and love,
by the sharing of what he calls his "glory":
"the glory that you have given me I have given them,
so that they may be one, as we [Father] are one,
I in them and you in me,
that they may become completely one,
so that the world may know that you have sent me
and have loved them
even as you have loved me" (17:22–23).

Because the Father lives in Jesus
and Jesus lives in us,

we are brought into holy communion
with both Father and Son, and that communion
creates our communion with each other.
The life and love shared between Father and Son
constitutes the Holy Spirit,
and this is the life and love they share with us.
Jesus' glory is the glory of us all.

This same Jesus, this same Christ
who lives with the Father in glory
and at the same time remains with us
till the end of time,
is celebrated daily in the Eucharist,
in this very church at this very time.
May we enter into holy communion
with our God and with each other,
in the breaking of the bread
and the sharing of the cup.

Friday

Love and Service

In Rome, where Peter was martyred,
in the church of Santa Maria del Popolo,
hangs Caravaggio's "Crucifixion of St. Peter."
Peter is seen lying on his cross
surrounded by executioners.
The cross is set at a diagonal
from lower left to upper right.
Peter's left hand, closest to the viewer,
appears to be already nailed to the cross.
But is it? On closer inspection
it seems that he is only holding the nail,
waiting for the executioners to drive it in.

This is the artist's way of depicting the spirit
in which his subject undergoes martyrdom:
Peter embraces it.
Tradition has it that Peter asked to be crucified head down
because he was not worthy to die
as his Savior had died.

In today's gospel what Jesus says to Peter
is intended as an indication of the kind of death
by which Peter is to glorify God:
"Very truly I tell you, when you were younger,
you used to fasten your own belt

and to go wherever you wished.
But when you grow old,
you will stretch out your hands,
and someone else will fasten a belt around you
and take you where you do not wish to go" (John 21:18).
In the movement of spirit which Peter must undergo,
there are two moments, just as there were for Christ.
In the first moment Christ prayed:
"[R]emove this cup from me."
But then in the next moment he says:
"[N]ot my will but yours be done" (Luke 22:42).

Peter's martyrdom brings to full term
that service which has its roots
in the answer he gives to Jesus' three questions.
Three times Jesus asks him: "Do you love me?"
Jesus requires of Peter three affirmations
in order to cancel out, so to speak, his three denials.
Peter is "distressed" that Jesus has asked him
the same question a third time,
but later he will gladly remember:
"I said 'no' three times,
but I said 'yes' three times too."

When Jesus first asks the question,
it contains a very pointed comparison:
"Simon, son of John,
do you love me more than these?" (John 21:15).
At the Last Supper, Jesus had said:
"You will all become deserters,
for it is written: 'I will strike the shepherd,
and the sheep will be dispersed.'"
At which Peter protested:
"Even though all become deserters,

I will not" (Mark 14:27, 29).
So now when Jesus asks:
"[D]o you love me more than these?"
Peter answers: "Yes, Lord; you know that I love you."
Each time Peter answers,
Jesus missions him to shepherd his flock.
Service must be rooted in love,
and it must grow out of love.

So it is with us: "Do you love me?"
If we say yes, we will do as he commands.
And what is his commandment?:
"Love one another as I love you" (John 15:12).
This makes our life, like Peter's, a life of service,
a service rooted in love and inspired by love.[46]

Saturday

Acts 28:16–20, 30–31
John 21:20–25

Come, Holy Spirit!

The seven times seven days of the Easter Season end today.[47]
Tomorrow is Pentecost, fifty days after Easter.
That's what Pentecost means, the fiftieth day,
the day on which we celebrate
the coming of the Holy Spirit,

[46]Adapted from the author's *The Paths of Life, Cycle C*, 74-76.
[47]*The Vatican II Weekday Missal*, 828.

the Spirit of Truth who "will be my witness,"
as Jesus said at the Last Supper (John 15:26 NJB).

Jesus tells his disciples
that they too would be his witnesses;
and in both readings today, the concluding words
of the Acts of the Apostles
and of the Gospel According to John,
we hear stories about three of those witnesses.
Two of them were martyrs, Peter and Paul.
The word "martyr" is from a Greek word for "witness."

Paul was under house arrest in Rome
for two full years, as we hear in the first reading,
but "with all boldness and without hindrance"
he was able to proclaim the kingdom of God
and teach everything he knew
about the Lord Jesus Christ (28:31).
That was certainly the kind of witnessing
that is first and foremost for every disciple.
His martyrdom, another kind of witnessing,
took place a few years later after a second arrest.

Today's gospel begins just after the risen Lord
tells Peter that he too would be martyred.
"Follow me," Jesus says. And now when Peter turns
and sees the Beloved Disciple, he says:
"Lord, what about him?" (21:19, 21)
Which is a way of asking,
"Is he too going to be martyred?"
What Jesus says, in effect, is that martyrdom
is not the only way to witness to him;
the Beloved Disciple will remain
and bear witness to him till the very end.

But will he die? Yes, of course.
According to Raymond Brown,
even after the death of the Beloved Disciple,
the Spirit of Truth "who bore witness
through and in him remains with all believers,"[48]
remains with each and every one of us.

Come, Holy Spirit, fill the hearts of the faithful,
and enkindle in them the fire of your love.

---

[48]*The Gospel According to John*, 29A, 1122.

In the Light of the Lord   193

Works Cited

Barclay, William. *The Gospel of John*, vols. I and II, revised edition. Philadelphia: The Westminster Press, 1975.

Brown, Raymond E. *The Anchor Bible: The Gospel According to John*, vols. 29 and 29A. New York: Doubleday, 1970.

_____. *The Gospel of John*, 12 Audio Cassettes. Wales: Welcome Recordings, 2000.

_____. *A Once-and-Coming Spirit at Pentecost*. Collegeville, MN: Liturgical Press, 1994.

_____. *A Risen Christ in Eastertime*. Collegeville, MN: The Liturgical Press, 1991.

Catechism of the Catholic Church, Second Edition. Libreria Editrice Vaticana, 1994, 1997.

Clare of Assisi: Early Documents, translated and introduced by Regis Armstrong. Mahwah, NJ: Paulist Press, 1988.

Dickinson, Emily. *The Poems of Emily Dickinson*, edited by R. W. Franklin. The Belknap Press of Harvard University Press, 1998.

Fallon, Michael. *The Winston Commentary on the Gospels*. Minneapolis: Winston Press, 1980.

Ferlita, Ernest, S.J. *The Paths of Life, Cycle A, B, C*. New York: Alba House, 1992, 1993, 1994.

_____. *Gospel Journey*. Minneapolis: Winston Press, 1983.

_____. *The Way of the River*. New York: Paulist Press, 1977.

Harter, Michael, S.J., editor. *Hearts on Fire*. St. Louis: The Institute of Jesuit Sources, 1993.

Hellwig, Monika. *Jesus the Compassion of God*. Wilmington, DE: Michael Glazier, 1983.

Hopkins, Gerard Manley. *Poems and Prose of Gerard Manley Hopkins*, selected & edited by W.H. Gardner. New York: Penguin Books, 1983.

Hughes, Gerard W. *Oh God, Why?* Oxford: The Bible Reading Fellowship, 1993.

Johann, Robert. *Building the Human*. New York: Herder & Herder, 1968.

Julian of Norwich. *Showings*, translated with an introduction by Edmund Colledge, S.S.A, and James Walsh, S.J. New York: Paulist Press, 1978.

Kent, Michael R. *Bringing the Word to Life*. Mystic, CT: Twenty-Third Publications, 1995.

LaCugna, Catharine Mowry. *God for Us: The Trinity and Christian Life*. HarperSan Francisco, 1991.

Lee, Dorothy A. & Honner, John, S.J. *Wisdom & Demons*. Richmond Victoria: Aurora Books, 1993.

Link, Mark, S.J. *Vision 2000, A Cycle*. Allen, TX: Tabor Publishing, 1992.

_____. *Mission 2000, B Cycle*. Allen, TX: Tabor Publishing, 1992.

Lorenz, Konrad. *King Solomon's Ring*. New Jersey: The New American Library, 1952.

MacRae, George W. *Invitation to John*. Garden City, NY: Image Books, 1978.

McKenzie, John, S.J. *Dictionary of the Bible*. Milwaukee: The Bruce Publishing Company, 1965.

McPolin, James, S.J. *John*. Wilmington, DE: Michael Glazier, 1979.

McTernan, Oliver. *A Call to Witness: Reflections on the Gospel of Matthew*. London: William Collins Sons & Company, 1988.

Meier, John P. *Matthew*. Collegeville, MN: The Liturgical Press, 1990. (Michael Glazier, 1980).

The New Jerome Biblical Commentary, edited by Raymond E. Brown, S.S., Joseph A. Fitzmyer, S.J., Roland E. Murphy, O. Carm. Englewood Cliffs, NJ: Prentice Hall, 1990.

Neil, William & Travis, Stephen H. *More Difficult Sayings of Jesus*. Grand Rapids, MI: William B. Eerdmans Publishing Company, 1981.

Peck, M. Scott. *People of the Lie*. New York: Simon & Schuster, 1998.

Rahner, Karl. *Biblical Homilies*. New York: Herder and Herder, 1966.

Ramshaw, Gail, editor. Richer Fare: *Reflections on the Sunday Readings of Cycles A, B, C*. New York: Pueblo Publishing Company, 1990.

Sanford, John A. *The Kingdom Within*. New York: Paulist Press, 1970.

Shea, John. *An Experience Named Spirit*. Chicago: The Thomas More Press, 1983.

Smith, Herbert F., S.J. *Sunday Homilies*, Cycle A. New York: Alba House, 1989.

Stanley, David M., S.J., *"I Encountered God!" The Spiritual Exercises with the Gospel of St. John*. St. Louis: The Institute of Jesuit Sources, 1986.

Stuhlmueller, Carroll, C.P. *Biblical Meditations for Lent*. New York: Paulist Press, 1978.

_____. *Biblical Meditations for the Easter Season*. New York: Paulist Press, 1980.

Tetlow, Joseph A., S.J., "Accurate Image," *America*, May 2, 1980.

The Works of St. Patrick, translated and annotated by Ludwig Bieler. Westminster, MD: The Newman Press, 1953.

In the Light of the Lord

Scripture Index

Old Testament

Genesis

15:1	*178*
17:3–9	*82*
17:4	*82*
26:24	*178*
37:3–4, 12–13, 17–28	*42*
45:5	*43*

Exodus

12:1–8, 11–14	*95*
32:7	*67*
32:7–14	*67*
32:11	*67*

Leviticus

19:1–2, 11–18	*21*

Numbers

21:4–9	*78*
21:9	*78*

Deuteronomy

4:1, 5–9	*52*
4:8	*54*
6:5	*56*
7:1–2	*32*
26:16–19	*31*
30:15–20	*15*

2 Kings

5:1–15	*47*
18:3–4	*79*

Esther

C:12, 14–16, 23–25	*27*
C:24:14, 23, 24	*27*

Psalms

16	*104*
16:11	*53*
18:6	*85*
23	*143*
36:9	*9, 147*
71:5	*92*
98:3–4	*155*
119:130	*9*

Wisdom

2:1, 12–22	*70*
21:16, 20	*71*

Sirach

28:2	*51*

Isaiah

1:10, 16–20	*36*
4:18–19	*48*

Isaiah (continued)

41:10	178
42:1	89
42:1–7	89
42:6	89
49:1	91
49:14	65
49:15	66
49:1–6	91
49:5	92
49:6	91
49:8–15	65
50:4–9	93
52:13–53:12	99
53:5	99
55:10–11	23
55:11	23
58:1–9	17
58:8–9	18
58:9–10	19
58:9–14	19
65:17–18	62
65:17–21	61

Jeremiah

7:9	73
7:23–28	54
7:28	54
11:18–20	72
11:20	73
17:5–10	40
17:10	41
18:18–20	38
18:20	38

20:10	84
20:10–13	84

Ezekiel

18:21–28	29
37:21–28	86
37:23	87
47:1–9, 12	63
47:9	64

Daniel

3:14–20, 91–92, 95	80
3:25, 34–43	50
9:4–10	33
13:41–62	75
13:60	76

Hosea

6:1–2	58
6:1–6	58
6:4	59
6:6	59
14:2–10	56
14:4	56

Joel

2:12–18	13

Jonah

3:1–10	25

Micah

7:14–15; 18–20	44

In the Light of the Lord

New Testament

Matthew		25:35, 40	18
3:17	89	25:40	94, 127
5:11	168	25:42–45	26
5:14, 16	168	26:6–9	94
5:17–18	52	26:14–25	93
5:17–19	52	26:21–25	93
5:20–26	29	26:27–28	39
5:38–39	30	28:8–15	103
5:43–48	31	28:16–20	175
5:44	31	28:20	108, 177
5:48	32	28:20	108, 177
6:1–6, 16–18	13		
6:7–15	23	**Mark**	
7:7	27	5:41	139
7:7–12	27	6:50	178
9:14–15	17	8:27	71
9:15	17	10:17–18	36
10:34	160	12:28–34	56
11:13	53	12:29–30	56
12:3–4	52	12:31	57
14:27	178	12–34	57
18:21–22	50	14:27, 29	191
18:21–35	50	16:8	113
20:17–28	38	16:9–15	113
20:19	39	16:10–11	114
20:21	39	16:13	114
20:22	39	16:15	176
20:26–28	40	16:15–20	175
21:33–43, 45–46	42		
21:42	43	**Luke**	
23:1–12	36	4:24	49
25:31–46	21	4:24–30	47

Luke (continued)

5:27–32	19
5:30–32	20
6:35	34
6:36	33
6:36–38	33
6:37	33
6:38	35
9:22–25	15
9:24	15
11:14–23	54
11:23	55
11:29	25
11:29–32	25
11:49–50	84
13:32	63
15:1–3, 11–32	44
15:20	45
15:31–32	46
16:19–31	40
18:9–14	58
18:13	59
22:34	51
22:42	190
24:13–35	107
24:31	108
24:35–48	109
24:36	109
24:39	109
24:44	109
24:46–53	175
24:49	175

John

1:14	23
1:43	153
1:43–51	73
1:45	153
3:1–8	115
3:5	115
3:7–15	117
3:8	117
3:14–15	78
3:16	79, 119, 167
3:16–21	119
3:19	121
3:31–36	121
3:36	121, 122
4:14	134
4:39	133
4:42	167
4:43–54	61
4:50	61
5:1–3, 5–16	63
5:17	65
5:17–30	65
5:31	67
5:31–47	67
5:35	68
5:36	68
5:42	69
6:1–15	123
6:7	153
6:16–21	126
6:20	178
6:22–29	129
6:26–29	130

In the Light of the Lord

John (continued)

6:30–35	131
6:35	131, 134
6:35–40	133
6:44	135
6:44–51	135
6:51	136
6:52–59	137
6:53	137
6:57	137, 138
6:60–69	139
6:61	140
6:64, 66	140
6:67–69	140
7:1–2, 10, 25–30	70
7:5	70
7:6, 10	70
7:28–29	71
7:37–39	116
7:38	64
7:39	115
7:40–53	72
7:48, 52	72
8:1–11	75
8:7	76
8:12	167
8:21–30	78
8:28	78
8:31–32	80, 81
8:31–42	80
8:33, 34, 37	81
8:37	80
8:51–59	82
8:56	82

8:58	82
10:1–10	140
10:5	106
10:9–10	141
10:11–18	143
10:14–15	143
10:15–16	144
10:16	185
10:22–30	145
10:28	145
10:29–30	146
10:31	85
10:31–42	84
11:45–56	86
11:47	86
11:49–50	86
11:52	87
12:1–11	89
12:3	90
12:7	90
12:21	153
12:44–50	147
12:46	147
12:49	147
13:1	96
13:3	23, 92, 95, 149
13:1–15	95
13:13–15	96
13:16–20	149
13:20	150
13:21–33, 36–38	91
13:34	164
13:36	91
14:1	152

In the Light of the Lord

John (continued)

14:1–6	151	16:20–23	177
14:5	151	16:22	178
14:6	73, 152	16:23	179
14:7–14	153	16:23–28	179
14:8	153	16:24	116, 180
14:9	154	16:29–33	181
14:10	46	16:30	181, 182
14:12	154	16:33	161, 182
14:16	175	17:1, 6	184
14:21, 23	120	17:1–11	183
14:21–26	157	17:3	146
14:22–23	158	17:11	184, 185
14:27	160	17:11–19	185
14:27–31	159	17:17–19	186
15:1–8	161	17:20–26	187
15:4	162	17:22–23	187
15:9	166	17:26	146
15:9–10	164	18:1–19:42	99
15:9–11	163	18:37–38	72
15:11	164	19:30	100
15:12	191	19:37	99
15:12–17	165, 166	20:11–18	105
15:13	87	20:17	106
15:15	106	20:18	106
15:18	168	20:27	123
15:18–21	167	20:29	110, 114
15:26	179, 192	21:1–14	111
15:26–16:4	169	21:12	111
16:5–11	171	21:15	190
16:7	172, 173	21:15–19	189
16:12–15	173	21:18	190
16:13	173, 179	21:19, 21	192
16:14–15	174	21:20–25	191

In the Light of the Lord

Acts of the Apostles

1:1–11	175
1:4	175
2:14, 22–32	103
2:22	103
2:28	53, 104
2:32	103
2:36–41	105
3:1–10	107
3:6	107
3:11–26	109
3:24–25	110
4:1–12	111
4:13–21	113
4:20	114
4:21	114
4:23–31	115
4:31	115
4:32–37	117
5:17–26	119
5:20	119
5:27–33	121
5:32	121, 122
5:34–42	123
5:41	123
6:1–7	126
6:2	129
6:8	129
6:8–15	129
7:51–8:1	131
7:55	132
8:1	132
8:1–8	133
8:26–40	135
9:1–20	137
9:31–42	139
9:40	139
11:1–18	141, 143
11:15, 17	142
11:17	144
11:19–26	145
12:24–13:5	147
13:13–25	149
13:16	149
13:26–33	151
13:32–33	152
13:44–52	153
13:47	154
13:52	154
14:5–18	157
14:11–12	157
14:19–28	159
15:1–6	161
15:7	165
15:7–21	163
15:22–31	165
16:1–10	167
16:11–15	169
16:2	170
16:22–34	171
17:15, 22–18:1	173
17:32–34	174
18:9–10	177
18:9–18	177
18:23–28	179
19:1–8	181
19:2	181, 182
19:6	181

Acts of the Apostles (continued)

20:17–27	183
20:22	183
20:23	184
20:28–29	185
20:28–38	185
20:32	186
22:30; 23:6–11	187
25:13–21	189
28:16–20, 30–31	191
28:31	192

Romans

8:26	179
11:17–24	162

1 Corinthians

2	173
10:17	112
11:23–26	95
11:26	97
15:9	133

2 Corinthians

5:18	29
5:20–21	14
5:20–6:2	13
5:23–24	29
6:1	14

Ephesians

1:17–19	176
1:17–23	175
1:20–23	176
5:8–10	9

Philippians

2:5	57
2:9, 11	92
4:5–7	28
4:7	161

Colossians

1:15–20	83

Hebrews

4:14–16; 5:7–9	99

1 Peter

1:3, 6, 8	12

In the Light of the Lord